HIGH INSIDE

HIGH INSIDE

Memoirs of a Baseball Wife

Danielle Gagnon Torrez
and
Ken Lizotte

G. P. PUTNAM'S SONS
New York

The authors gratefully acknowledge Jeanine Duncan for
permission to reprint lines from her poetry, copyright © 1983 by
Jeanine Duncan.

Library of Congress Cataloging in Publication Data

Torrez, Danielle Gagnon.
  High inside.

  1. Torrez, Mike. 2. Baseball players—United States—
Biography. 3. Torrez, Danielle Gagnon. 4. Wives—
Biography. I. Lizotte, Ken. II. Title.
GV865.T65A33   1983   796.357′092′4 [B]   82-25546
ISBN 0-399-12786-0

PRINTED IN THE UNITED STATES OF AMERICA

ACKNOWLEDGMENTS

Like baseball, a book is a team effort. We especially thank Sonny Trapilo, who initiated the idea for *High Inside,* and Michael Snell, who developed it into book form. Our editor, Diane Reverand, provided the guidance which always kept us in the game.

Of course, the first team consists of all the baseball wives. Good friend Liz Mitchell stands out among the many who shared experiences with us: Cindi Roberts, Bev Stock, Jeanine Duncan, Sharon Hargrove, Anna Moskau, Connie Robinson, Betty Howe, Audrey Chambliss, and Jackie Dark.

Brooks Robinson, Paul Mitchell, Wes Stock, Alvin Dark, and Dan Kinder helped add the male perspective. Special thanks to Association of Professional Ballplayers of America Secretary-Treasurer Chuck Stevens for putting us in touch with so many baseball people.

No project like this could succeed without the folks who work behind the scenes: Phil Gibbons, Rick Hoyt, Jean Renard, Bill Kramer, Gary Provost, Deborah Valianti, Carmen Parizeault, Josh Gordon, Susan Snell, Mike McDonough, Nancye Araneo, and Ed Lizotte.

to Milou, with tears behind and greatness ahead, together

—D.G.T.

to my parents, who were patient

—K.L.

CONTENTS

HIGH INSIDE

PROLOGUE

In June, 1980, a few months after my separation from Red Sox pitcher Mike Torrez, I got a phone call from my friend Jeanine Duncan. We'd first met in 1975 when Mike and her husband Dave had been teammates at Baltimore. Now, years later, she was still married while I was settling into a life on my own. I had a three-year-old son and plans for a new career. When she called, I'd been sitting in my new apartment wondering how to start.

"Jeanine, where are you?" I asked. "In what part of the world?" With a wife of a ballplayer, you never knew.

She laughed. "I wish I were *somewhere,*" she said. "But I'm home in Arizona, with my baby and my mother." She had just had her first child.

"What about Dave?" I asked.

Her voice got flat, almost annoyed. "Dave's been gone for six weeks," she said, "since the opening of the season. It's his second year as a coach in Cleveland. I'll probably join him when he locates an apartment up there. But I refuse to live in a hotel again like last year." Her voice softened and trailed off. I remembered the wives' arch villain—the road—all too well.

It was great to hear Jeanine's voice. She'd been a terrific friend, the kind who, despite pain of her own, would always be there if you needed her. And at this point, I really did. I'd been feeling very abandoned. Few of the other wives ever called. When you divorce baseball, someone once said, baseball divorces you. It was as if I'd betrayed them, the other wives. I'd not stuck it out, not abided by the rules. So, at the sound of Jeanine's familiar voice, I got very nostalgic. I'd not realized how much I'd missed her. I began to cry.

"Oh, Jeanine," I said. "Sometimes, it's so tough . . ."

"I wish I could be with you," she replied. "I know it's been rough leaving Mike. But think of what you have: a place of your own, a beautiful son, the career you've been longing for." Then she paused. "And your soul."

My soul, I thought. Yes, I did have my soul. But I wanted my husband, too. I'd just returned from a week in the Bahamas, an attempt to get as far away from him, and my feelings for him, as I possibly could. I'd even met a tall, handsome man there, and he'd tried his best to distract me. But I couldn't imagine getting close to someone new. For six years, my life had revolved completely around my husband and his very consuming, inescapable world. But even after a separation and the beginnings of divorce, I still felt "married." In my mind, I was still Mike's wife.

We had met in '72 in Montreal. I was nineteen and he was twenty-six. We'd been of the same mind, then, the same hopes: a bright future together, a happy family, two caring partners, each with fulfilling, stunning careers. Immediately after our marriage, we'd begun a steady climb to the top: five different major league clubs in six years, Mike's salary and notoriety up a notch at every step, our fast-paced life together growing in leaps and bounds.

Ultimately, it had changed things between us. Mike, it seemed, shunted aside his earlier values. He began partying more often and making excuses for those who drank, popped pills, had extramarital affairs. This scared me and even made me suspicious. And created a very high, very thick wall.

It all flooded back now, as Jeanine spoke: Mike on the mound for the Yankees, October 18, 1977. Yankee Stadium, sixth game of the World Series. Eight to four, Yanks ahead, final inning, two outs. Los Angeles Dodger outfielder Lee Lacy at the plate. Mike begins his windup, cocks his big right arm, throws. Lacy slams at the ball, but only pops it up, the highest pop-up I'd ever seen. With 54,000 other Yankee fans, I wait for the fall. Over a hundred thousand eyes looking to the sky. My husband under the ball. *My* husband.

Then, all at once, screams of delight, the ball plops with finality into his glove! It's over: behind the pitching of *my* husband, the New York Yankees have won the World Series!

I was paralyzed with joy, couldn't speak or think. Manic excitement exploded all around me. My husband had won the game, the World Series! *My* husband.

At this time in our marriage, Mike and I had everything: a luxurious penthouse with a spectacular view of New York; a stately powder-blue Cadillac; and constant attention and adulation from fans, including gifts like cases of fine wine and even, once, a two-week vacation to Hawaii. In December, Mike would sign a multiyear contract with the Boston Red Sox for three million dollars.

The parade of famous players who became our friends was astounding. Reggie Jackson, Lou Piniella, Carl Yastrzemski, Rollie Fingers, Willie Davis, Vida Blue. But behind the scenes, they were as human as anyone else: Jim Palmer with his cockiness and superstitions, Bill Lee with his off-the-wall ideas, easygoing Brooks Robinson with the same constant,

15

modest homelife, despite superstar status, for over twenty years.

There was that dark side of baseball, too. As the wife of a ballplayer, I'd been expected to live in Mike's shadow. When we'd first married, I'd already had a thriving career in Montreal as a fashion model and TV commentator. After the wedding, there was great pressure to give it all up, to stay home, to raise a family. A large family.

Marilyn Monroe had felt the same pressure. Though Joe DiMaggio had retired more than two years before their marriage, the pull of this powerful sport refused to let him go. He and Marilyn would sit at Toots Shor's in New York for hours with Joe's friends. Cigar smoke, raucous laughter, statistics and scores. As dazzling as Marilyn was in those days (and she was at her height), Joe, said many, was even bigger. His legacy, it seemed, would never die.

Once, Marilyn entertained some troops in Korea—a hundred thousand wild, exuberant male fans. She returned home, ecstatic, and cried, "Joe, Joe, you've never heard such applause."

In his quiet, dignified way, he replied, "Yes, I have."

Soon after, he started asking her to retire from the screen.

"Why can't you be like the other wives?" Mike once said to me. "Why can't you just stay home with our son? Forget your career: why would anyone want to hire you for an important job, anyway?"

All the emotions ran through me then: confusion, rage, heartbreak. I'd rooted for him from the stands, consoled him after difficult games, treated him for injuries, and defended him against both fans and the press. I remembered also picking up at a moment's notice after trades and abandoning friendships, familiar surroundings, attempts at a career. I had really gotten behind him, in the process leaving so much of myself far behind. But one day, it was all too much. There was nothing left to do but get out.

Now, months after our separation, I was slowly making the adjustment. I'd lost a husband, the dream of a family, a father for my son, and I'd lost "the life." For eight years, I had known little else but marriage and baseball. I shivered suddenly, very scared.

"I don't know, Jeanine," I said. "At times, I have very bad moments."

"Oh, I just wish I had your courage," she said. "Look at me: as rough as this life can be at times, I know I could never leave. But *you're* doing it. Oh, Danielle, how can you live without baseball?"

I wasn't sure. For all its trials, simply to be a ballplayer's wife had felt so special. It'd become as much a part of me as Mike himself. On my recent trip to the Bahamas, I'd kept checking the box scores.

One day, I read a quote from Mickey Mantle: "Ever since I retired, I keep having these dreams. The worst one is I go to the ballpark late, jump out of a cab, and I hear 'em calling my name on the public address system. I try and get in and all the gates are locked. Then I see a hole under the fence and I can see Casey looking for me, and Yogi and Billy Martin and Whitey Ford. I try to crawl through the hole and I get stuck at the hips. And that's when I wake up, sweating."

I knew I'd made the right choice, though. Living with baseball had meant living with so much anxiety. I could only speculate how things might have worked out had Mike been a plumber or schoolteacher. No groupies, no road trips, no childish demands. But even so, in some ways, I still envied Jeanine Duncan intensely.

"I get real mixed up at times, Jeanine," I said. "Sometimes

17

I wonder who really has more courage: wives like you who stick with it or wives like me who get out."

"I love you, Danielle," Jeanine said, "and I know you can go on. I'm sure that sometimes getting out is the only way. But a lot of the wives don't even believe it can be done. Please win for me and for all of us, Danielle. Show us it can be done."

"I'll try," I said. But as I hung up, I thought again about the past eight years. That life had been so damn thrilling. And I thought, too, about Mike, about his loving eyes in our early years together, his great tender smiles. Giving up both him and his world had been like ripping out a part of me.

But at least, as Jeanine said, I now had my soul. . . .

ONE
MONTREAL

December, 1972, Mike Torrez waited inside the doorway to Harlow's, a chic Montreal discotheque, looking like a helpless little boy. People struggled to get by, but he seemed not to notice. It was the first time I'd ever laid eyes on him. I was surprised at his size: six-foot-six, massive shoulders, huge hands at the end of log-shaped arms. He was unlike all the other men entering Harlow's for the party. Most were shorter and very thin and seemed like men who got plenty of rest. Bankers, executives, pampered media stars, playboys, lawyers. Men who, even at work, sat around a lot. Nothing physical.

Unlike Mike, they dressed smart: tapered double-breasted jackets, wide lapels, wide ties or turtlenecks. Fabrics like wool, gabardine, camel hair. They looked like fashion ads in *Esquire*.

In contrast, Mike wore a beige polyester shirt open at the neck, a burgundy jacket, and a pair of double-knit slacks with black-and-white checks, little cubes, crisscrossing up and down his legs. He could have been a golf pro who had not quite figured out the look. He just didn't fit in.

"Was that supposed to be your blind date?" my escort, Pierre, asked.

"Must be," I whispered. I usually came to these affairs with Pierre, but he'd been out of town the last few days. This was a special reopening party for Harlow's, only VIPs invited, and I'd wanted to go but felt uncomfortable attending alone. So a friend had matched me with this Mike Torrez.

"You don't have to stay with him if you don't want to," Roger said on the phone. "Just use him as your escort to come in the door."

Then Mike called. I was hesitant to go with him at first. He wanted to meet me for a drink first, and I wasn't sure I wanted to do that. As Roger had suggested, I really only wanted to use him to get in the door. But as he talked, I warmed up a little. He had a slow, gentle sound to his voice. So I agreed to meet him.

As soon as we hung up, Pierre called. "I'm back in town!" he announced. "I'll pick you up for the Harlow's party in half an hour." I told Pierre I'd call Mike back and cancel the blind date.

"My boyfriend's back in town," I told Mike. "I hope you don't mind."

"I understand," he said graciously. "Maybe I'll see you there."

We hung up.

But when I saw him at the door, I was embarrassed. Maybe it was his choice of clothes, or maybe it was just that feeling you sometimes get when you don't know someone. Nervous anticipation. No matter, I looked up at him as he looked down at me. But like shy little kids, we let the moment pass. Mike quickly turned away, and Pierre and I went inside.

For me, this kind of party was very familiar. Harlow's was a tribute to Jean Harlow, with blow-up stills from her movies, Tiffany lamps, velvet love seats, and marble-topped tables.

The dance floor was sectioned off by glass walls and by a gigantic floor-to-ceiling mirror. The whole place was like a very tasteful speakeasy of the twenties and thirties, and its management had recently spent three months making it sparkle. It would be a showplace in Montreal for the next several years, until closing its doors in the late seventies.

While Mike stuck out awkwardly among the men, I fit in very well with all the women. I wore black gabardine pants, a white silk wraparound blouse with a black sash, and black patterned platform shoes. The women at Harlow's could all have posed comfortably in store windows. They knew precisely how to look.

I was comfortable with these people, these corporate professionals, wealthy socialites, local celebrities. I'd been working and playing with them for some time. Though still in my teens, I was already a well-known fashion model, and I'd also co-hosted a trendy TV interview program called "Pop." At the age of sixteen, I'd been formally engaged to a dashing journalist named Claude Poirier. Claude had known everyone in this clique and had introduced me to them all. I'd met musicians, artists, fashion designers, news commentators, politicians, and people of wealth. He'd taken me to gala balls, prestigious awards presentations, and little high-brow bridge parties and teas. But the fifteen years difference in our ages was responsible for the breaking of our engagement.

Three years later, though, I was quite well-known. At nineteen, I was Danielle Gagnon, bright, blond, and fashionable, a hometown teen fashion queen. It was a role that had come easily and that I'd never questioned. I loved it.

I recall dancing a lot at Harlow's that night. Pierre was an actor and producer and loved to talk theater. He hated to dance, though, so I danced with others. As the evening went on, I began to realize that wherever I was in the room, Mike was watching me. He slinked around posts and craned his neck during conversations. If I went whirling out onto the dance floor, his eyes followed me around. If I ended a dance in a new corner of the room, he moved to a better viewing area. This huge foreigner even banged his head on a hard overhead umbrella shade and tried to act as if nothing had happened. By then, he knew I was watching him back. He just rubbed his head and made a bashful shrug.

Near the end of the evening, a woman who I didn't know walked up and asked. "Are you Danielle Gagnon?" I said I was.

"Someone wants to meet you," she said and waved in Mike's direction.

He came toward me, getting bigger and bigger as he lumbered across the room. Then he smiled and nervously said, "So you're Danielle?"

I smiled back. "You're Mike Torrez?"

He leaned over and kissed me on each cheek, the European way. But all he did was kind of smack my cheeks and smudge my makeup. I didn't care.

"You're a popular girl," he said. "I've been watching you dance. Thirteen partners!"

He was good-natured and without affectation. If he was straining to impress me, it didn't show. He seemed bare, stripped down somehow to his essentials. I felt a very faint, curious tug.

"Who do you know here at Harlow's?" I asked. I couldn't imagine how a character like this could get invited to something so exclusive.

"I know the manager a little and a couple of the bartenders. I used to come here on the weekends sometimes after a game," he said. "I'm a ballplayer."

"Oh?" I said. He didn't look like a quick and wiry ballplayer, like the soccer players I knew. "What kind of ball?"

"Baseball," he said. "With the Expos. I'm a pitcher."

Suddenly, I knew him. Mike Torrez. Yes, indeed, Mike Torr-rrez. I was really embarrassed, but he couldn't know why. I recalled a Saturday afternoon the previous summer when my father had been watching a game on TV.

"I don't understand this game," I pouted. "I want to watch something else. How can all these grown men spend so much time chasing a little white ball around a field?" My father, an enthusiastic sports fan, refused to look at me. He just shifted in his big easy chair. He knew my act. He was one of those grown men who spent lots of time watching these other grown men chasing a little white ball.

"Today's pitcher," said the announcer, "is new Expo Mike Torr-rrez." He rolled his *r*s like a Spaniard.

Ah, my next line of attack. "Oh, Torr-rrez," I mocked. "Mike Torr-rrez, Torr-rrez, Torr-rrez." My father, with the dignity of a palace guard, ignored me even more.

Tonight that same Mike Torr-rrez was standing before me and asking for a date. "Could I call you tomorrow?" he asked. "Could I see you tomorrow?"

He seemed so much like Clark Kent: probably very strong and competent underneath, but somehow too mild-mannered and clumsy up front. Still, for some reason, I was beginning to like him.

"Tomorrow?" I said. "Yes, why not? Call me around noon."

He thanked me, bowed, and walked away.

A short time later, I swept into my parents' bedroom and woke them up.

"You'll never guess who I met tonight," I said, bouncing onto my parents' bed. My mother awoke immediately. My father only half opened his eyes. It was not customary for me to do such a thing, to wake them up over a new man. But for some reason, I was suddenly very excited. I leaned down and placed my mouth close to my father's ear. "Mike Torr-rrez," I

23

droned softly. Then I burst out laughing as my father bolted straight up in bed.

"The baseball player Mike Torrez?" he said.

"Yes, the baseball player," I said. "And guess what? He's calling me tomorrow. He may even be coming over tomorrow."

"The baseball player Mike Torrez?" my father said again. "Coming here?" He nearly leaped out of bed right then to begin getting ready.

I awoke the next morning to a raging blizzard. Snow had begun falling after I'd left Harlow's and had never stopped. Even in a city so accustomed to winter storms, this one was slowing everyone down. But Mike called and insisted he come over anyway. I gave him directions in my best English, which was quite poor, and prayed. Montreal, with its many bridges, interchanges, and superhighways, is one of the easier urban areas in which to get lost. Mike's apartment was in the heart of Montreal, and our house was only fifteen minutes away in a little suburb called Chateauguay. But you had to know how to get there.

I'd directed him to meet me in a parking lot a few streets from my house. I waited in my little yellow Pinto reading that morning's newspaper, then started a crossword puzzle on another page. Soon, the snow had enveloped my wheels and began piling up rapidly around both bumpers. Fifteen minutes passed, then a half an hour. "My goddamn English," I muttered. "He's probably in Quebec City by now."

An hour later, I was still waiting, and more and more snow created shifting mountain ranges across my hood. I had been so sure he would come, but he was now more than an hour late. He had either given up or had taken one wrong turn too many. One thing for sure: he wasn't coming here. I turned on the ignition and put my Pinto in gear. As I released the brake, he drove up.

24

He had a big clunky Chrysler, very tacky in deep maroon with white trim, a kind of old person's car. Big and cumbersome, just like him. On the side of the car, some hand-painted lettering read, "Courtoisie de La Salle Chrysler." My ex-fiancé Claude had also driven such cars—vehicles provided gratis to budding celebrities in return for the promotional value of the sign. For new stars like Mike or Claude, it was not a bad deal.

He leaped out of his car, rather nimbly I thought for someone so big, and traversed three snowdrifts to my car.

"Well, I made it," he said, huffing.

"Are you all right?" I asked, rolling down the window. "Did my directions confuse you?"

"I took a wrong turn, yeah," he shrugged. "But I'm here. What now?"

He didn't seem upset, but he admitted later he actually was. He'd exited at not one, but two mistaken ramps and had gone far out of his way. When he finally pulled into the parking lot and saw me comfortable and snug in my little yellow car, he'd boiled over. "This broad isn't worth it," he'd thought. But since he'd finally made it, he decided he might as well make the best of things.

Minutes later, we were at my house. We walked in, and my father lit up at the sight of Mike, charging at him with an outstretched hand. "Welcome, welcome," he said in English. He almost knocked Mike over with the smell of his cologne. So excited about meeting a real live baseball player, my dad had spent all afternoon getting ready. He'd showered and shaved—twice!—and splashed on cologne. He'd prepared the fireplace, then dashed on a little more cologne. He carped at my mother all afternoon to prepare some nice food, and in between hounding her, he'd poured on even more! In the past, I'd dated actors, TV newsmen, men of wealth, once

25

even a baron. But for none of these men had my father used so much cologne.

"Come in, come in, let me take your coat," he said. He wrestled with Mike's heavy overcoat, eventually subduing it near the closet. Meanwhile, my mother, who spoke no English, kept nodding shyly. Very nervous, she whispered to me in French. "He's even bigger than I thought." Mike spoke Spanish, but no French, and I guess was as nervous as she. "Hello, madame," he kind of boomed, as if talking to someone who was deaf. Weakly, my mother nodded again.

My father monopolized things for the first half of the evening. He asked all kinds of questions about baseball, while my mother stayed in the kitchen cooking ham. Meanwhile I sat at a table with my father and Mike and tried to look involved. Finally, the four of us gathered in the kitchen to eat. My father kept asking Mike questions, and at one point Mike looked at me and gave a little shrug. Then his eyes locked on me, a slow and very fond stare. With his long legs jutting out from beneath the table, I thought: he's like a big, stuffed teddy bear. Wrong wrapping, of course, not pink like the one sitting in my bedroom, but, all in all, very sweet and cute.

Finally, a hockey game came on TV, and my father rushed to the den to see it. My mother went back to the kitchen, and Mike and I moved to the living room. He began saying how impressed he'd been the night before. "You had so many men watching out for you," he said, "protecting your virtue. I wondered what you were like, what you'd done to win these guys over." I smiled, not knowing how to answer.

He asked if he could see me again. I said yes. He wasn't my type for anything long-term, I was sure of that, but I thought, why not try him for another date? We agreed to see a movie the next night.

He had a little trouble leaving, though. Backing his big Chrysler out of the driveway, he plunged firmly into a huge

26

snowbank across the street. Fortunately, my father, ever ready to do a favor for his new friend, the baseball star, scrambled out into the street with the biggest snow shovel I'd ever seen.

Mike looked sheepishly at my mother and me, my father frantically shoveling the snow in all directions. "We don't have snow like this in Kansas," he drawled.

Finally, my father was finished, and Mike pulled away. "See you tomorrow," he said as he drove off. Then, we all watched as his big funny car slipped and slid all the way down our street.

The next night, dinner and a movie. *The Godfather* had just opened, but I couldn't quite follow the dialogue. Too much English. "What'd he tell her?" I whispered. "What was that word?" I kept pestering him through the first reel, and he finally told me to just shush.

"I'll tell you after," he said. "Watch the movie."

I felt slightly rebuffed, but not much. My English was just so bad. The night before, I was telling Mike about an uncle of mine who was retired. I'd said "retarded."

"Ohh," Mike said softly. "That's too bad."

"Oh, no, it's great!" I cried cheerfully. "He's been retarded for two years now. He loves it!"

Another moment, intending to ask him if he'd gotten a hangover from the Harlow's party the night before, I said, "You seemed to drink a lot. Do you have a hang-up?"

After the movie, Mike took me to a wonderful restaurant with a medieval decor. It had stone arches, drapes with silk ropes, and a small stone fountain in the middle of the main dining room. The owner's family crest was carved in wood and hanging over a fireplace. Mike and I sat in high-backed wooden chairs, just like royalty five hundred years before. Mike was particularly pleased with the roominess of his seat.

27

"I guess they realized back then there'd one day be big men," he said.

The waiter came and Mike tried to pronounce his selection. I laughed condescendingly at his clumsy French, then read my own choice in English. Such a suave, little, sophisticated bird I was: "Chief's salad," I said confidently. Even the waiter laughed at me.

Despite the language barrier, we did converse. We found out, at once, how different we really were. While I'd grown up an only child near the high fashion and cultural diversity of Montreal, Mike had lived with seven brothers and sisters in a cramped wooden house in a Mexican neighborhood in Topeka, Kansas. Neither of us had been born rich, but our parents lived in very different ways.

In my case, my parents had wanted to provide me with all they could. As a result, they had often gone without certain amenities, say, a dining room set, a house with a backyard, and, for a time, even a car. Our income was very limited: my father was a bus driver and my mother a part-time waitress, but they'd always seen to it that I had a fresh, stylish wardrobe even if my mother herself could afford only one or two good dresses of her own. They also bought me a cozy white-framed bed, a tiny white bureau, a miniature china tea set, and many, many dolls and stuffed bears. If I was deprived as a child, I never knew it.

My parents also instilled in me a self-image of being pretty and special. They were strongly determined to improve things. Our future, my mother always said, was within our control. But at all costs, even if they couldn't manage it for themselves, at least their daughter would have a fair chance.

By contrast, Mike's family was far too burdened to scheme or plan. Survival was their loftiest goal. Their house, for example, was creaky, old, but very clean. It was in a deteriorated section of town and even lacked plumbing. Just a narrow outhouse in the yard out back. Mike and his brothers grew out hunting jackrabbits, which their mother would skin and cook for dinner. Everyone did chores at home and worked at odd jobs around town. They gave no hard thought to the future. How different could it possibly be from today? Why think about it? But despite all, there was always plenty of love and laughter.

A switchman for the railroad, Mike's father had about as good a working class job as a heartlander could find. Especially a Mexican-American in Kansas. But even on union wages, he undoubtedly had a rough time feeding a family of nine.

Mike explained how one day the hand of fate had rescued him from all this. He was about fifteen and had been working with his brother Johnny in the hot sun picking potatoes one afternoon on a nearby farm. Their boss, the farm's owner, paid them a dime a bushel. If they worked hard and fast, they'd fill six or seven bushel baskets an hour. In the dustbowl in the early sixties, this was about as good a summer job as a teen could find.

This particular day it was hotter than usual, and Mike and his brother began to ache. "Our backs were usually the first to go," Mike said. Then the fingers would dry up and the skin begin to crack. And the dust would clog up the lungs. Pretty rough.

A practical joke usually helped. So this day Mike sneaked up behind Johnny with an extra-large tater.

"Hey, Johnny," he snickered softly. "Ya hungry? How about a nice, cool spud!" He yanked at his brother's beltline and dropped the potato inside.

Johnny retaliated at once. He picked up one of Mike's full baskets and dumped it over his brother's head. Then, they both went tumbling to the dirt. Minutes later, they were sprawled out and giggling atop mounds and mounds of tossed potatoes.

"TORREZ!!" boomed the farmer. "Quit horsin' around!" They both looked up to see him standing over them, his coveralls grimy, a craggy scowl on his hard, brown face. "I pay you boys to work!" he snarled.

He stomped away across the rows. Mike reached for one of the larger taters and weighed it in his right hand. "That no good son of a bitch," he muttered. He curled back his arm and pursed his lips. The farmer was moving steadily away, thirty paces, now forty. "And for a crummy half buck an hour." He slung forward his arm, fast, and the jagged oval sailed very straight, whistling through the air. Just as the farmer climbed up on the back of a truck, the tater slammed square on the back of his leathery neck.

"Holy shoot, Mike!" yelled Johnny. "You done knocked him down!"

Their boss wasn't out, though, just dazed, and he sat up very slowly, rubbing his neck. Then he squinted toward the brothers through the heat. He'd flipped backward right off the truck.

"You're home early boys," he growled weakly.

"We finished early!" hooted Johnny, as they scampered away.

An hour later, Johnny excitedly told their father what Mike had done. "Shoulda seen that spud whip across the field, Pa—like lightnin'!"

The man just listened, then waved Mike outside. "Go on out back, boy," he said. "We're gonna play us some pitch."

Though the worlds in which we grew up were very different, our solutions were not. Just as Mike soon realized where his fortunes lay after he discovered pitching when he was a teenager, I also learned early in life that my looks might be the key to something better. My mother had gotten

30

me started by placing a strong emphasis on neatness and discipline.

In addition to a sparkling house, this meant keeping our appearances immaculate. It was her belief that with the proper attitude we could rise above our financial limitations. And if she and my father couldn't manage it themselves, at least their daughter might have a chance.

As early as age four, I'd been totally conditioned. I was sitting in a row of metal chairs with fifteen other children on a stage right as a school play was about to begin. Just before the curtain opened, I noticed a pesky fold in my dress. I quickly stood up to fix it. The little boy in the next chair gasped.

"Well, I have to make myself pretty," I retorted. Then, as I finished, the curtain opened and the audience began to applaud. They were clapping for the opening curtain, but I didn't realize it. I assumed they were clapping for me.

"See?" I said proudly. Then I curtseyed to the audience and sat back down.

In the seventh grade, the plot thickened. I attended Villa Marie that year, a boarding school run by a convent of nuns. I loved everything about Villa Marie, from the daily smells of baking bread to the chapel with its tiered chandeliers, from the great beige harps in the music rooms to the beautiful antique clocks, from the stained glass window panes to the spring flower gardens. And we students, too, had a particular look and feel: heavy brown shoes, navy blue cashmere sweaters and skirts, and wide white collars that had to be snapped on and off and washed nearly every day. Even our hair ribbons were regulation: again navy blue with little cotton ridges running up and down. Far from repelling me, this regimentation made me very proud. I was a part of something, of a particular set of values one could actually see. My uniform was the most visible statement: your appearance is a lantern

to the world, it reflects inner light. Care, precision, hard work.
I wore it with zest.

I was thirteen when I left Villa Marie. By this time, it
seemed almost preordained I'd become a model. Hanging
clothes on myself had become second nature. What's more, I
loved it, whether pretty, little-girl party dresses, or sober, precise school uniforms. When, two years later, my mother casually mentioned modeling school, it had an immediate appeal.
I knew, if nothing else, I wanted someday to be special. I'd
seen far too many girls become stagnant, imprisoned: pregnancy, then marriage, then the death of dreams. I could even
see my current teenage friends already heading there. I
wanted something more.

For six months the next year, I attended modeling school.
Molly Saks, the owner of the school, taught us everything:
how to walk as if on egg shells, how to pivot, how to move our
hips just a half-step before our shoulders, how to hold our
heads high and straight while on the runway. This last one
was my shakiest—I was always so scared I'd fall. Molly constantly yelled: "Danielle, if you look down as you walk, I
guarantee you'll fall!" How right she was! Despite her advice, I
continued to peek—and to tumble off the stage.

One day, I got my first chance to test what I'd learned. My
mother had been on the phone talking excitedly, and when she
got off, she grabbed me and pushed me into the bathroom.
"Get ready now, _très vite._ Hurry!" she said. "You've been
offered a good job! At Wonderbra! You must go at once!" I'd
been offered my first modeling assignment—a one-day photo-
graphic shoot for a bra advertisement.

My father drove me to the studio, but soon disappeared
behind the photographer's bright lights. On arriving, I'd been
shown a very sassy framed photograph on the lobby wall.
"That's the look we want," one of the advertising men told
me. He had black horn-rimmed glasses, a short crew cut, and

a dark blue suit. I looked at the photograph: it was of a well-known, but very snobby, Montreal *modèle*. The other girls at the modeling school all hated her.

"It's a vampy look," the ad man said. "We like that."

A half-hour later, they'd put so much makeup on me, it felt like an acre of loam. Someone held up a mirror and I jumped back. Was that me? I was fifteen when I walked in here; I now looked forty-five!

"Perfect!" snapped the ad man.

"Wonderful!" cried the bra exec.

I was positioned behind the lights. "Turn this way," someone said. Then, "Oh, no, the wire is showing! Turn more to the left, more, more . . ." Lots of whispering—all men's voices and all in English—and more commands to turn. I was very confused, and also half-naked in a big, drafty room. And blind from the bright lights.

"Look comfortable!" someone yelled. "You must look comfortable!" But this wonderful brassière of theirs was jabbing me in the ribs! Its wires would surely leave a scar or two; I was already bruised. More whispering behind the lights. What were they saying?

"There's a fold in one of the pads!" the ad man suddenly cried. "It's not smooth anymore, it must be smooth!" Panic scampered through the room. I straightened up, gave them the most fierce, disapproving look I could imagine. I tried to show exactly how I felt about all of them. Revulsion.

"Magnificent!" came a joyous response. "You've got it exactly! Now hold a minute . . ."

They were all very pleased.

When Mike and I first met, I didn't realize how all-encompassing his career really was. One night, in a restaurant, he ordered quails, six tiny birds on a big oval platter. As he ate, he looked to me like a gangly, tender giant. His size and his physical ability were cute and comic. Only gradually did I see they were much more.

We were once visiting my father's family in Chicoutimi, a rugged lumberjack region some three hundred miles north of Montreal. It was January, and since snow remains there until well into spring, it was all very white.

"Do you ski?" I asked Mike.

"No," he said. "I'm not allowed."

"Not allowed? Not allowed by whom?"

"It's in my contract," he answered. "I can't ski or play football or anything else that might endanger my arm." He rubbed lightly his right bicep and smiled. "This ol' muscle of mine is valuable, you know. For the Expos, it's a big investment."

Mike explained to me then how that was so. He'd been spotted in his teens by a "bird dog," a retired ballplayer or ex-coach who scouted small towns for new talent. The bird dog who discovered Mike worked on commission for the St. Louis Cardinals.

"Wow!" cried the bird dog, watching Mike pitch one afternoon at an American Legion ballfield in Topeka. "Move over, Bob Gibson. Have I got a comer for you!"

At the time, Bob Gibson was a fast-rising right-handed pitching star with St. Louis. He'd been improving steadily the last five years, and talk around the National League was that he'd soon be setting records. He was the showpiece of the Cardinals. This Mike Torrez, at age seventeen, looked just as promising. So the bird dog dropped a dime in the nearest pay phone and called the front office at Busch Stadium. Before long, Mike had a bonus of $20,000 simply for signing and a base pay of $600 a month. The investment had begun.

Before he could actually play in the majors, he had to pay dues. He was assigned to a "farm team," so-called because he would be prepared there—cultivated—for the major leagues.

34

For the first three years of his contract, he played for teams in North Carolina, Arkansas, and Oklahoma. By the end of the three years, the Cards decided he was ready. In August of 1967, Mike put on his first major league uniform. "Cardinals" was scrawled across his chest below two pointy-headed red birds. As he told me all this, I could only imagine how he must have felt. A lanky young Chicano from Kansas found himself in the dugout with faces from bubble-gum cards and names from box scores in the *Topeka Capital-Journal*. Orlando Cepeda, Steve Carlton, Curt Flood, Lou Brock. Even the man who topped the Babe, Roger Maris. Names headed for Cooperstown. And Gibson, big Bob Smoking Gibson, with massive biceps and that pouty, almost frightening stare. What was the son of a poor railroad man doing there among all these greats? How long could he last? The Cardinals had already won one recent World Series (1964) and seemed destined for two or three more. What was farm boy Mike Torrez doing there at all?

I asked him what he felt. He began relating a childhood incident, so at first I thought he'd misunderstood my question. He'd gone to a girlfriend's house one summer night, he said, to pick her up for a date. He knocked on her front door, and her father came out but stayed behind the screen.

"She's not goin' with you," he growled. "You can just go on home. No damn wetback's gonna date my daughter." Then he slammed the big wooden main door in Mike's face.

"I sat in the dugout that day," Mike said, "and I thought: what would her father say now?" He leaned back in the chair and stopped talking and the air in the room suddenly got very stiff. Before he told me this story, I'd never seen him in a low mood. He'd always been cheerful, congenial, up. He never got angry and never bothered with controversial subjects like politics or religion. But after saying this, he got very quiet. A dog started barking outside, and I heard a church bell resound

35

from a mile away. It's OK, I thought, I'm here with you now. I put one hand lightly on his arm. We stared at the wall.

After a while, he continued. He'd spent five years with the Cardinals, mostly on the bench, then was traded to Montreal. He hadn't proved himself yet, he was still learning, so the move to the Expos was really for the best. At that time, Mike was like the Expos organization itself: young, relatively new to the league. Only two years before, the Expos had been formed. They were the first team from a foreign country to be added to the American baseball leagues. Mike was one of their first prized additions. They nurtured him like a racehorse. His owners hoped that one day there'd be a super payoff. The gate, the bell, the fast clip, the surge. At the final turn, extend. Mike Torrez, Montreal's front-runner. No skiing, no football. The finish line and the pennant drive in September. Their major investment.

Back then, when he told me all this, I couldn't see it. When we'd met, baseball was just one topic, only a component, in our conversations. Baseball players have lives of their own only three months of the year: November, December, January. That coincided exactly with our first months together, so I was not to see how consuming baseball could actually be until early February. At that time, Mike invited me to spring training.

"Oh, that sounds like fun," I said naively. "What day is it?"

He laughed and pulled me close. "It's not a day, hon, it's two months: February and March. And it's in Florida. A lot of the guys will have their wives there and a few of them will have girlfriends. I'd like you to come."

We'd only known each other for two months. I wasn't sure about him yet and I was still taking our relationship from date to date. But even these thoughts didn't really matter: I knew my parents would never approve.

"Let's try and convince them," Mike said.

So, I mentioned it to them, but as I'd expected my mother

said absolutely not. My father agreed: "Out of the question," he said. Then Mike suggested that maybe they'd change their minds if we pushed for only one month. But it was still no.

"How about a week?" Mike said. "A weekend?"

But they kept saying no.

"You don't really know him yet," my mother said. "Besides, you're not married." The matter was closed.

When I saw him off at the airport, I wished I'd fought harder. As he walked down the ramp, I suddenly had the strongest desire to go with him. But I wondered, too: is this what being with a ballplayer is all about? Two months away every spring? I'd have to drop everything—work, social events, family, friends. And for what?

Mike called nearly every day from Florida. He would tell me things on the phone I couldn't understand. Baseball jargon, too new and complicated. I'd begun to read the sports pages every day but the big picture was slow to sink in. "I walked two in the fifth," he'd say, "but snagged a pop and forced an out at home." I had no idea what he was talking about. He tried to explain it sometimes, and I'd listen and pick up what I could. But I was really reading the paper as much to see his name and his photograph as anything else. It seemed so important to him to be telling me all these things that I let him ramble. And slowly this strange game seeped in.

In April, he returned. I fantasized a romantic scene outside the airport, the wind blowing madly at our hair, and both of us rushing headlong, feverish, into each other's arms. But it didn't happen that way. He just ambled down a ramp with a fat gray athletic bag and his usual big wide grin. He was darker than ever.

"You're so tan!" I said as I stretched up on my toes to hug and kiss him.

"Well, you would be, too," he replied, "if you'd have been

there." Then he threw his big arm completely around me and we walked away.

As the season began, I was quite proud. Six months ago, I'd known nothing about Mike's profession. Now I knew quite a lot. Or at least I thought I did. Two teams got nine turns each to score the most points. Simple, right? I'd also learned many baseball terms: runs, or in French, *les points;* hits, or *les coups sur;* innings, *les manches;* outs, *les retraits;* and homeruns, *les coups de circuit.* I also knew the titles of players' positions: Mike was a pitcher, *le lanceur,* and there was a catcher, *le receveur,* and players at first base, *le premier but,* second, *le deuxieme but,* and third, *le troisieme but.* The shortstop was *l'arrêt-court,* and the outfielders were *les voltiguers.* The manager, *le gérant,* ran the whole team.

I knew also that, at the end of the season, first place teams in both the American and National Leagues won "pennants," and these slim little flags represented the league championships. They then played each other in the World Series. I also learned that baseball was one of the most grueling sports because the schedule—162 games—was so long, and that Montreal, being a newer team, would probably not win many games this year but was, instead, "building" for the future.

The season opened in April, and I was eager to attend my first game. "Well, you can come to the opener if you want to," Mike said, "but I won't be pitching. Are you sure you won't be bored?"

No way, I said. I really wanted to be there. So he got my father and me complimentary tickets.

At the game itself, I was taken by surprise. I expected only a serious, competitive event. What I got instead was a circus: vendors in the aisles hawking popcorn and ice cream; billboard displays for Coke, Molson and smoked meat; a little organ playing jaunty sing-alongs; and ballplayers in pristine white suits cavorting over a bright, expansive green field. There had been a multicolored wooden booth at the front gate where a man in a pink pin-striped vest disbursed tickets. An usher had directed us toward a grandstand and another usher pointed high up toward the topmost seats.

"Section Nine," he said, handing us back our stubs. "Family section."

My father and I looked up. Way up there?

We climbed about thirty rows and took seats under a white wooden press box. I could see radio and TV commentators wearing headphones. They shuffled papers and squinted through binoculars at the field. From up here, we could easily see the whole park: gray-metal bleachers in right field, concrete grandstands in left, and dark green chain link fencing which rimmed all the rest. Jarry Park, or *parc Jarry*, was a municipal playing field. Until the Expos, it had been used primarily for high school events and for semipro football and soccer. With a capacity of only 30,000 fans, it was nonetheless the largest "stadium" around. Since I knew nothing of the grander parks, like those in Cleveland (capacity: 76,000) or Philadelphia or Anaheim (both 65,000), to me, *parc Jarry* was like a huge coliseum. I even got upset when Howard Cosell came to town a month later and referred to it as that "cute little French park." Who was this big, snobby American, anyway? (I'd never heard of him.) How dare he snub my park?

But though I didn't realize it, my mistaken impressions were just beginning. I thought I'd taught myself quite a lot. I soon learned otherwise. A tall, chubby man in a black suit waddled onto the field and stooped over home plate. He pulled a little whisk broom from his back pocket and began to dust.

"Oh, that's nice," I said. "I guess it's his job to keep everything clean."

My father looked at me. Was this dumb daughter of his

really serious? "That's the umpire," he said gruffly, studying me. "He's only dusting the plate so it will be easier to see. He calls the balls and strikes."

Danielle Gagnon: no hits, one error. Next, I scanned the field for Mike. The other players were batting balls and sprinting across the field and playing catch. After a while, Mike sauntered out and began to peer up into the stands.

"There he is," I said, nudging my father, "he's trying to find us!" I got very excited, I could tell he couldn't see us, so I began waving my arms. When he saw me, he gave a perfunctory wave and then frowned. He kneeled down on the grass and lightly punched the ground. It was a signal I interpreted as, "Sit back down." I wondered what I'd done. After the game, he explained, "You were flapping your arms like a wet seal. Couldn't you see the other women in your section? Baseball women don't act that way."

I had seen the other women all right, but I hadn't been entirely sure who they were. They were all young, in their early twenties, sitting in twos and threes, and occasionally alone. There were few men among them, and they all talked quietly and kept their eyes on the game. Unlike many of the other fans, none of these women seemed to get excited. Also, I never saw any of them look my way, though I sensed they knew I was there. I thought I caught one of them peeking at me from the corner of her eye. But there was nothing overt. I sat almost exactly in the middle of Section Nine and I might as well have been invisible.

As the game began, my mistakes continued. In the first inning, a third baseman dove for a hard line drive and made the catch. "Yayyy!" I wailed, jumping from my seat. But none of the fans in the surrounding section cheered with me. My father looked upset.

"Why isn't everyone happy?" I asked. "That was a great play . . . wasn't it?"

40

"Sure," said my father. "For the other team!"

Then, in the third inning, the Expos fell behind. That other team, the Phillies, slammed three hits: a double and two singles. The Expos were now behind 1–0, with runners on first and third. The Expos' manager, Gene Mauch, walked slowly out to the mound. The catcher, John Boccabella, joined them. The three stood there for a couple of minutes quietly chatting.

"Why don't they play?" I said. "Why are they wasting time?"

"They're not wasting time," said my father. "They're strategizing."

"But why don't they strategize *before* the game?" I asked. I wanted action!

"They can't. There are too many possibilities. They have to wait and see what happens and figure things out as the game goes along." He laughed. "When you understand things better, you'll realize this is one of the most exciting parts."

I couldn't believe him. I thought hits and homers were what you came for. Pitchers' duels and second-guessing seemed a bore. I remembered coming home one afternoon the summer before and finding my father in the middle of watching a game on TV. Though baseball didn't interest me, out of idle curiosity I'd asked him the score.

"Nothing to nothing," he said. "Sixth inning."

"Oh," I said. "Nothing's happened yet."

Today, I was not much better. Finally, Mauch left the field and Boccabella returned to the plate. The game resumed. The next batter, outfielder Greg Luzinski, a big bear of a man, took a mighty swing but only tapped the ball toward first base for an easy out. The fans around us went wild. *"Il est mort!"* they screamed. *"Il est mort au premier but!"* Literally, this means "He is dead at first."

"Mort?" I said. "He's dead?"

41

"Only in French," my father chuckled. "In English, they say, 'he's out.'"

In the fifth inning, I noticed Mike sitting on the top step of the dugout and making notes in a little black book. Other people in the stands were doing the same thing. "What are they writing?" I asked.

"They're keeping score," my father said. He handed me his program. "Here, you try it."

I looked at a page filled with tiny boxes and diagonal lines. There were instructions, but they got real complicated, real fast. "Oh, I can figure this out myself," I said cockily. I looked at the scoreboard and began marking everything down. A few minutes later, I'd come up with the score: Expos, 590, Philadelphia, 212.

"Something's wrong," I thought, and looked at the scoreboard again. I circled the first digits in each of my scores. Hmmm. That was more like it. I'd been copying down far too much. I'd been grouping together runs, hits, and errors. Since the Expos had five runs, nine hits, and no errors, I'd recorded 590!

But my scoring of the actual plays was even worse. There was nothing to check it against: I couldn't ask my father— he'd suffered enough—so I just kept it up. When the catcher caught a foul ball in the sixth, I wrote down "12," the number on his jersey. I didn't realize I should have written his "position" number. For scoring purposes, baseball designates players by position: pitcher, 1; catcher, 2; first base, 3; second base, 4; third base, 5; shortstop, 6; and outfielders, 7, 8 and 9. A double play, then, from shortstop to second base to first, is 6–4–3. Mine was 19–16–28. Needless to say, when the game was over, I had one weird, if highly original scorecard. There were large numbers, crisscrossed lines, and entangled diagrams. Mike looked at it in the parking lot after the game and tried not to laugh. But he couldn't keep it in. He was soon doubling over and slapping his thighs.

"I'm sorry, hon," he said. "I just think it's so cute." He gave me a kiss and a hug, but was soon giggling away once more. "Don't worry, you'll get the hang of it." Then he laughed and added, "Eventually."

The next day I saw Mike pitch for the first time. I knew he'd be on the mound, but I was still too much of a novice to understand what this meant. How long would he be there? One inning, two innings, the full nine? Pitchers seemed always to be coming and going throughout the game, and at this point, I still had no idea why. My eyes roamed the field. I realized with a start that Mike was standing on the mound. I watched his big, tall, seemingly cumbersome body. He raised his arms, leaned backward, pivoted at the hips, and quickly snapped forward. He did this again and again, and it was very graceful. Such a delightfully smooth movement, I thought, like a dancer. After seeing his clumsiness on the dance floor—he always jerked around as though his body was too difficult to maneuver—I was impressed now with how well-coordinated he was on the field. My boyfriend was at the center of the action and as smooth and confident as a swan. I wanted the world to know he belonged to me.

As the summer wore on, I began attending games with Carmen, my longtime friend. Mike continued to provide the tickets, so Carmen and I came to every game like two carefree, bubbly college girls. Carmen was a striking platinum blonde who I'd known since my early teens. She was one of those friends with whom you could really share the cloudiest, murkiest secrets and the brightest, most thrilling joys. About the game itself, though, she knew less than I.

At a twi-night doubleheader, a few weeks later, we both got

a lesson. After nine full innings, the score was tied, 3 to 3. "What happens now?" Carmen asked.

"They play extra innings!" I said. "Until someone scores."

"What happens if no one scores?" she said. "Is there a curfew?"

I didn't know. By now, I'd seen two or three extra-inning games but they'd both ended in the twelfth inning. What if the game went longer?

"Someone will score," I said, trying to sound confident. "At least, I hope so."

By the twelfth, however, no one had. Innings thirteen, fourteen, fifteen. Still 3–3. Mike was normally a starting pitcher, but by the sixteenth, the Expos had run out of relievers. In came Mike.

"I thought you said someone would score," Carmen said. It was midnight now, and we were both cold and tired. And this was only the first game!

"I want to go home," she said. One inning later, I said the same.

In the top of the eighteenth, it began to rain. The score was still 3 to 3. A fan behind me started rooting for no one to score. "If it goes to twenty-two, we'll set a record," he announced jubilantly. History never looked so unimportant.

Finally, in the bottom of the eighteenth, at 2 A.M. EDT, the Expos scored. The damn game was finally over. Montreal had used every pitcher on its roster, even the pitching coach. There'd been no curfew, though the second game was mercifully postponed. I kidded Mike after the game.

"I'm never going again," I said. "Never."

He laughed. "Neither am I."

In time, I became familiar not only with how the game was played, but with who played it best. When one of the league's superstars came to town, I soon learned enough about him to be both awed and frightened. One particularly intimidating player was Pirate outfielder Willie Stargell. In '73, he led the National Legue in both home runs and runs batted in, so whenever he came to the plate, especially against Mike, I'd cover my face with my hands. I always expected him to hit it out of the park, to defeat the Expos all on his own. And frequently, that's just what he did.

Another played who scared me to death was Hank Aaron. The slugger with the Braves was, by this time, an historic figure. I first saw him in 1973, when he was very close to breaking Babe Ruth's long-standing record for career home runs. Early the next year, he did it, hit home run number 715. He was one of those players that Mike and the other Expos had looked up to in their youth: legendary quick wrists, unassuming, affable manner. The essence of the dignified, intimidating hero.

At one game, Mike was giddy with joy because he managed to get Aaron's autograph. This enthusiasm infected me, too, and I decided I wanted to shake Aaron's hand. But I was confined to Section Nine and forced to sit tamely in the stands and just watch him running around in the outfield. But when his turn came to bat, I had the same fears as with Willie Stargell. I was filled with awe.

Another batter who amazed me was Pete Rose. At this time, he'd been an outfielder with the Reds for many years and he wound up leading the league in 1973 in batting with an average of .338. Though I admired and respected his talent, I was a little upset with his style. Where Aaron and Stargell seemed very neat and dignified, Rose was wild, excessive, overbearing. Many of the Expos nicknamed Montreal shortstop Tim Foli "Crazy Horse." This tag fit Rose much, much more. When Cincinnati came to *parc Jarry,* Rose spent the whole time chugging and bounding up and down the field. He hustled down the base paths, slid headfirst into bases and home plate, and leaped and tumbled while chasing long fly balls. I kept thinking of the French word, *zèle,* meaning zeal. Pete Rose, it seemed, had much too much.

On the other hand, many of the pitchers in the National League were just the opposite. Two I admired in particular were the Phillies' Steve Carlton and the Mets' Tom Seaver. Each seemed extremely classy on the mound and calm, upright, steady. I always felt as though a Pete Rose would do absolutely anything to win or to claim an advantage, while a Carlton and a Seaver had their limits. Mike admired them for this, too, and for their expertise. They seemed "well-educated," he said, not from books or from a classroom, but from careful and considered on-the-field studies of the league's batters and of their own strongest skills. Both Seaver and Carlton, Mike said, could really finesse a batter. They could reach down into some magical pocket and produce, when necessary, a clever and sparkling move. Mike respected that, and he admitted that he hoped one day he might be able to achieve such capabilities himself.

During my first year with baseball I also learned that Mike, being both a pitcher and a Mexican, was something rare. Until 1947, in fact, being anything at all in the major leagues except a pure white man was all but impossible. After '47, however, infielder Jackie Robinson became the first black man to play "organized ball." Immediately, baseball began signing up other nonwhites, chiefly American blacks and Latins from countries like Cuba, Mexico, and the Dominican Republic. Prior to this, there'd been a few Latins who had played, but not many. But more important, hardly any had been allowed to pitch. And long after 1947, it seemed, whites still controlled the action. One of my first impressions, in fact, at *parc Jarry,* was that white players occupied the infield and the mound, while black players were usually way out in the outfield.

Fortunately, I never heard any racial slurs hurled toward Mike from the stands. I did know, however, from what he told me, that it had been part of his past. Growing up in Kansas, he'd heard them all. Wetback, dirty Mexican, hondo, greaser. Because of this, it was important to him to prove something as Jackie Robinson had fifteen years before. He knew someone of Mexican descent could do this job, and he wanted to prove it once and for all. At all costs, he would certainly try.

Years later, of course, young Fernando Valenzuela would do exactly that. Only twenty years old and ignorant of English, Valenzuela would be discovered by a scout for the Dodgers in a ramshackle desert village called Etchoahuaquila, hundreds of miles from the nearest large town. Valenzuela was very fat and had had little formal schooling, but he would pitch so well his rookie year, 1981, that he'd win both the Cy Young Award, baseball's highest pitching honor, and also Rookie of the Year. No player in history had ever won both in the same year before. Valenzuela would prove to one and all that a Mexican's ability could match, and surpass, that of any white.

In the meantime, though, this new boyfriend of mine would help pave the way.

In the stands at most every game, Carmen and I were quite a sight. Being models, we often came wearing the most sparkling new styles. Among the players' wives, this really set us apart. Once, I wore a fluffy white fur coat, while Carmen wore red fox. We couldn't really afford these clothes, though we could often buy them at cost. Sometimes clients, as in this case, gave them to us outright. Like Mike's Chrysler, a client's clothing on a model around town was good for promotion.

The wives, however, dressed very differently. It was spring, 1973, and women in Montreal were wearing deep red nail polish, linens and silk, shag hairstyles and natural backward flips. These Americans sported light pink nail polish, polyester from head to toe, and thick, lacquered beehives and ringlets around the face. Ankle-baring slacks and miniskirts were out, but some of the wives still wore them.

I wasn't sure why this was. Were Canadian and American styles that different? Or did it have more to do with low salaries or with simple ignorance of fashion? I really didn't know. But the result was that Carmen and I stood out like well-heeled sore thumbs!

I also noticed the wives did everything in slow motion. As I'd observed that first day, they rarely got excited. The exception was when their husbands came up to bat or pitch. Carmen and I were like goofy schoolgirls. We laughed, spilled Cokes on each other, rooted and cried. Really had fun. But the wives did none of this. With them, each game was like a job.

As Mike's girlfriend, I was never invited to any wives' activities, like baby showers, luncheons, small parties, or even a fashion show!

"You're only a girlfriend," Carmen said. "Maybe if you become a player's wife, then you can join the club," she said.

So I settled for second best: I made friends with players' girlfriends. I became close to one in particular, a brash and vibrant Californian named Amy. In 1974, she arrived in Montreal with Willie Davis, an outfielder acquired in a trade with the Dodgers. Davis was a tall, muscular black who had been a star in California for many years. He'd played in three World Series, was consistently among the league leaders in hits, and had twice led the National League in triples. For a young team like the Expos, Davis was a treasured possession. As a result, he lived in luxury: $100,000 salary, a complimentary Lincoln, and free rent on a beautiful new home.

I was dazzled by Willie and Amy at first. They were wild and uninhibited. They wore expensive avant-garde styles and knew all the latest trends. Amy had a flushed, racy sweetness, a mixture of California sun and New York sass, a personality at once cheerful and tough. She was blond, had a face like Olivia Newton-John, and wore clothing she'd bought at Bloomingdale's—extravagant articles like cowboy boots, headbands, bright-colored beads, and designer jeans (long before the craze). Once, she came to a game wearing faded cut-off denim shorts and a purple suede vest with nothing underneath. A tiny gold cross hung on a gold chain around her neck. She was a bizarre addition to Section Nine, to say the least. She outshone Carmen and me by a mile. But I was glad to have her.

She once took me to Willie's house. We'd been shopping and had stopped by in the middle of the afternoon. We entered the living room, but I couldn't make out a thing. Dark, heavy drapes kept out all sunlight, while a shag rug, murky and chocolate-brown, stretched to all the walls. When my eyes adjusted, I saw an elaborate wooden altar. It was an eerie sight: I hadn't seen such a spiritual setting since my days at Villa Marie. Tall red candles, intricately carved figurines, a statue of Buddha, the fragrant aroma of incense.

"Willie's favorite room," Amy said. "He meditates here before every game."

We went into the bedroom. Filling up the center of the room was a gigantic round bed, with a pink satin comforter and frilly pillows. This room was also dark but in a different way—the sun filtered in through pink blinds, and its rays kind of lolled around on top of things. The general appearance could only be called magnificent clutter: baubles and rich clothing were everywhere, on the bed, across the floor, covering the dresser. There were shoes, dresses, designer jeans, dozens of makeup canisters, diamond earrings, gold bracelets, and blouses with crazy, psychedelic prints. There was also crinkled-up money, bills folded or compressed, ones, fives, tens, twenties. Amy began pushing them aside on the dresser as she searched for a hairbrush.

"How do you like these pants I bought?" she asked, holding up some silk palazzos. They were hand-painted in shocking pink, bright yellow, and a touch of aqua. "Would you wear pants like these?" she asked.

They weren't really my style, but they thrilled me. "They're beautiful," I said. "I suppose I would." It was out of the question, though; I could never afford them.

"Here, they're yours," she said. She tossed them toward me, and they landed on the bed. I just stared at them.

"What do you mean?" I said, not believing her. "Why would you give them to me? Don't you want them?"

I had never known her to be anything but in high spirits. But she suddenly sank down and dropped to the edge of the bed. She sat there for a while staring at the floor.

"No, I don't want them," she said slowly. "I don't want any of this." She looked around at the glitter and wealth. It was like a flea market on the Rockefeller lawn.

"You know what I do want?" she said. "I want a child." She looked up at me. "But Willie's already been married once. He's got two children now and he doesn't want another."

Amy had everything: money, fine things, a celebrity amour, an exciting life. I had a sudden vision of all her jewelry as fetters and chains. What she really wanted was a child. I didn't know what to say.

Then, all at once, she jumped up, alive again. "Let's go downtown," she said, grabbing my arm. "I think I need a new pair of boots." She was back now, the Amy everyone knew. We hurried to her little Mercedes and sped away.

As time went by, I finally got to know a few of the wives. The first was Diane Stoneman, whose husband Bill was a starting pitcher just like Mike. We were invited to a dinner party at their home, and I was impressed that, for a young couple just starting out, they could already afford such a nice house. Veterans like Willie Davis with their superstar salaries were one thing, but how much could a relatively unproven player like Bill Stoneman be making? It was not an extravagant house, just a pleasant three-bedroom contemporary. But it was more than I would have expected. "When you join the club . . ." I remembered Carmen's words.

Soon after, I met Steve and Sandy Renko. Steve was also a pitcher and he and Sandy not only had their own home, but were also raising two kids. I watched everyone in their family glide through the house, communicating directly and honestly and being very considerate. I liked that, saw a satisfied glow around them all. Steve and Sandy were pure and innocent and very giving. It was a relationship I enjoyed watching.

I also admired Sandy because she was one of the few wives who could talk about things other than diapers. I'd eavesdropped on many wives' conversations and had had a few myself, and I'd gotten tired of hearing about Lydia's newest cute word or little Peter's magnificent traverse in the kitchen. I liked kids, but there were limits. With Sandy, it was actually possible to discuss music, films, the news, even ideas. She also taught me a little more about baseball, but was never condescending, which she certainly could have been, since I still knew so little. I'd asked questions of some of the other wives, and they had made me feel stupid. But Sandy always treated me with great tact. She was like a star veteran player. If I ever did try out for the "club," using Sandy as a role model could insure that I made the cut.

One thing bothered me about Sandy Renko, however: she lacked a career. By the middle of '74, I was thinking about marriage. I still wasn't certain, but I was speculating like mad. I had to wonder if I were to marry a ballplayer, would a career of my own even be possible? Before I'd met the wives up close, I hadn't considered it.

I was bothered even more when I remembered Patty Foli. She'd been married to Tim Foli, the Expos' shortstop, and she was the third wife I'd gotten to know. At first, she seemed as content and unquestioning as all the others. She genuinely seemed to love baseball and was crazy about Tim. In fact, for a while, the only time I'd ever seen her upset was at a game in which Tim got rammed by a runner. The player had been trying to prevent a double play, so he just barreled right into Tim, hoping he'd drop the ball. You could hear the impact from high up in Section Nine. Tim dropped to the dirt like a dead weight, and Patty leaped from her seat. Before we could calm her, she tore away toward the dugout, climbed over a high dividing wall, and rushed to Tim's side. They carried him off to the clubhouse, and he recovered the next day, but I will never forget the anguish on Patty's face, her mounting terror. Like the most loyal of mates, she had sprung to him at once.

Later in the season, in September, she revealed something else. She was standing with me and the others in the parking lot of Jarry Park after a game. There was no wives' lounge, so we usually had to wait outside. Since we were often talked-out by now, these moments could be awfully boring. This particular late afternoon was cold and, worse, the game had run long, to eleven innings. We all just ached to go home. Suddenly, out of the blue, Patty said, "I'm so sick of this baseball thing."

Everyone got quiet and kind of blinked. It was the first time many of us had heard such a comment from a player's wife. Confused, I said, "Patty, I thought you liked baseball?"

She looked away. "I do. It's just . . ." She gazed back toward the park. "I'm just tired, that's all."

A week later, when the guys were the on the road, I called

her to see how she was. I was worried about her. Since her outburst, she'd seemed in very poor spirits.

"Would you like to stay over at my house some night?" I asked. She hesitated, then accepted half-heartedly.

She came over the last night of the road trip. We sat in my living room, watching TV. She was fine at first, then got very quiet. Suddenly, she said, "I think I'll go home."

I looked at her. "I thought you were staying?"

She listlessly stared at her knees and flicked away imaginary dust.

"The guys will be back tomorrow," Patty said. "I want to go home and bake Tim his favorite cookies."

She never explained to me what was really bothering her, but I knew one thing: Patty Foli was the first wife I'd met who'd seemed imprisoned by it all. Being a model baseball wife apparently didn't solve things. I even wondered if it might have made things worse. Would Patty have been better off if she'd had a life, or a career, of her own? Could it be she'd spent too much time thinking and worrying about Tim?

During the '74 season, things between Mike and me blossomed. His job, in particular, had become important to me, and I found it difficult at times to separate one from the other. Mike was baseball, baseball was Mike. Throughout the '74 season, I began taking this for granted. Occasionally I even gave him advice.

I'd heard this was dangerous, though. Players had a habit of ordering their wives or girlfriends, early on, to mind their own business. "Don't ever tell me how to do my job," was a common command.

It was sometimes wise to be cautious about discussing the game at all. One story I'd heard concerned the player who came home one day as his wife was making stew in the kitchen. Their radio had been out of order, so she wasn't able to listen to the game. With a huge grin, the player said, "OK, honey, ask me how things went today. Go on, ask me." His wife, seeing her husband's good mood, said, "All right: how did things go today?"

The player grinned even wider. "I got *five* hits: two home-runs, two doubles, and a single. I scored four runs, and we won the game, 5 to 3!"

The next day, the player, on returning home, didn't look nearly so good. But without waiting for her cue, his wife asked again. "Well, honey, how did things go today?"

The player spun around on his heels, and the look on his face could've startled King Kong. "Listen," he snarled, "let's make a deal: you do the cooking in this family, and let me worry about the baseball."

As usual, Mike was different. He rarely got mad at me, so I wasn't afraid to give advice. In July, I noticed he was throwing too many poor pitches. He kept tossing far more balls than strikes. I also noticed most of his bad pitches drifted far to the left.

"Why don't you try turning your body to the right before you pitch?" I said. "Maybe then the ball will also go more to the right and it'll sail right in for a strike."

Mike laughed and patted my head. "OK, Miss Fashion Model," he said. "But I think you better stick to clothing styles and I'll think about baseball."

The next day, however, he came out of the clubhouse like an embarrassed lamb. "Now don't get too cocky when I tell you this," he said, "but guess what the pitching coach just advised me to do?" More than any time before, I now felt an actual part of this game.

About this time, I found out how a team, on the inside, really worked. During winning streaks, for example, I learned that all the players would be in a constant state of optimism. The mood in the locker room would mushroom, Mike said, into great confidence. "What are we gonna do to win today?" was the kind of thing that was said.

During losing streaks, just the opposite occurred. Everyone would be sullen, unsociable, introspective. On everyone's mind was the thought, "I wonder what's going to defeat us today?"

I learned also about how players psyched themselves up for a game. It was mainly an individual thing, Mike said: players would get a little quieter or a little harder to talk to. They would start thinking about what was to come, concentrating on going onto the field, on statistics, on the swing of the wrist, a feeling in the arm. How to make it all come together, how to relax and make it all work.

Sometimes, managers helped them out. Tom Lasorda of the Dodgers was considered one of the best for motivating and psyching up his players. He could zero in on a player's personality and make just the right comment to perk him up and push his thinking in the proper direction.

Players also took special care not to downgrade a teammate in a slump. Every player knew that bad games and even bad seasons were inevitable. Sometimes, a player might offer advice to a slumping teammate, but most would simply keep quiet and let a teammate's difficult period take its course. Taunting or scolding was out of the question.

At the games, I paid particular attention to catchers. I knew that they had perhaps the toughest job of all. Simply bending down as they did throughout the game was difficult enough, as was wearing the extra equipment—face mask, chest protector, and shin guards. But, in addition, a catcher had to know the personalities and styles of all the team's pitchers, as well as understand the batters on opposing teams. It was the catcher's role throughout the game to give the pitcher advice by signaling, for example, with one finger for a fastball or two for a curve, or perhaps flapping his palm between his legs for a pitchout (a pitch far to the outside). It would then be up to the pitcher to accept or reject the advice by shaking his head no or nodding yes.

I learned, too, about conversation on the mound. "It's always things like how to pitch to the next batter, or how the pitcher's arm feels, or whether he's tired," Mike said. "It's never small talk."

Sometimes, though, a manager's main purpose for going to the mound is nothing more than to slow a pitcher down. Oakland manager Alvin Dark used to do this constantly with Catfish Hunter, for example, since it was the only bad habit Hunter had.

"Cat was so definite," Dark said. "He always knew exactly what he wanted to do. But sometimes he'd get ahead of himself, which made him a little wild. I'd have to walk out to the mound and say, 'Hey, Cat, let's slow down a little bit now!' And he always would!"

Finally, I learned, too, about how pitchers felt when Mike's manager, Gene Mauch, took them out of the game for poor performance.

"Does a pitcher ever refuse to leave?" I asked Mike.

"No pitcher *ever* wants to leave," he replied. "But the manager's always the boss." Pitchers sometimes insist that they're feeling all right, but almost never, Mike said, does a pitcher seriously object.

After learning so much about the game, I realized one day how much a part of me Mike and baseball had become. We were back at Harlow's, the nightclub where we'd met, and Mike said, "What would you do if I got traded?"

The question seemed silly and I said so.

"But would you come along with me?" he asked.

"Of course not!" I blurted out. Then I thought: why did I

say that, is that what I really feel? Mike raised both eyebrows when I said it, then became very quiet. Finally, he said, well, guess what, he really had been traded to San Diego.

I thought: what will I do now? Could I model in San Diego? Would I like California? Or the United States?

"What are you thinking?" Mike asked.

"I don't know," I said. "What we're going to do about this, I guess."

Then Mike got very buoyant and threw his arms around me. "Don't worry," he said. "I haven't been traded at all!" He said he just wanted to see if I cared.

"Well, of course I care," I said, more confused than ever.

Mike brushed back my hair and looked me in the eyes. "Well, honey," he said in his Kansas drawl, "*Jah t'aime*, too."

After this, marriage to Mike became quietly inevitable. I felt more and more ready to spend my life with him, wherever and whatever that involved. There was no formal proposal, as there had been with Claude. When I was sixteen, I hadn't been able to understand what marriage was. I now realized it was an extremely large, long, sometimes lonely commitment. With Mike, I wouldn't be merely watching my husband go off to work in the morning and greeting him when he came home. I'd sometimes go with him!

As we began to plan the marriage, Mike almost immediately asked me to sign a prenuptial agreement. For ballplayers, this was getting to be a common practice. During the course of a marriage, ballplayers' salaries could escalate sharply, so their lawyers had begun advising them to protect themselves in case of divorce. Mike's friend and teammate, outfielder Kenny Singleton, had already gotten his own fiancée, Colette, to sign such an agreement. And we'd all heard of another Expo whose fiancée wanted an agreement of her own. Upon any divorce, she demanded an allowance for herself and for her daughter from a previous marriage, as well as a half-interest in the players' current business holdings. Mike said if this player went ahead and married her, he'd be crazy, and I agreed. All these financial demands missed the point, I thought: if two people were truly in love, as Mike and I were, planning for divorce was self-defeating. It was making a firm commitment that mattered.

We double-parked Mike's car outside his lawyer's office and left its blinkers on as we hurried inside. I couldn't let this take too long since I had a fitting for my wedding dress in twenty minutes. There was a clause which prohibited any kind of financial settlement in case of divorce. Yet, none of this mattered to me—I'd be married to this big American the rest of my life. Mike was just doing what he was told, following the advice of his lawyer. So, without even reading it, I signed.

By this time, Kenny Singleton had married Colette, a stunningly beautiful woman with long auburn hair, who, like me, was a native of Montreal. Colette and I had something in common apart from baseball—we were both local girls. Since most of the other wives were from the U.S., we were among a very few in Section Nine who didn't long for the season to end. We were never homesick, as they were. We were already home.

Colette had a gift for making everything around her look beautiful. She could wear any style and make it her own. Her apartment was always sleek and well-coordinated, everyone's ideal. Like me, she had a strong attraction to elegance.

We were both dismayed, then, when we attended the wedding reception of one of the players. It was colorless and stark. The long rectangular tables and dull-white tablecloths reminded me of a banquet at high school. There were no flowers and few decorations. The meal was chicken à la king, and there was no band. We couldn't understand why the player's new wife had not planned something more elegant. Baseball

58

players were at least minor celebrities, and thus in the spot-light of the local media. Surely, the couple would want to present a favorable image. What they'd arranged instead did not seem right at all.

Later Mike explained. The couple had been offered a pack-age deal by the restaurateur, a deal too much a bargain to refuse. The restaurant would be taking a loss on this recep-tion, but hoped to make it up in publicity. It was the restau-rateur, then, who had planned their arrangements. And like any businessman, keeping costs down was number one. As we all raised our glasses for the traditional toast—white wine, there was no champagne—I assured myself that my own re-ception would not be like this.

A few days later, though, Mike and I got a very similar offer. This restaurant owner (a different one) wanted us badly. I'd always dreamed of holding my wedding reception in an elegant hotel ballroom with glistening chandeliers and a stun-ning gold decor. I certainly didn't appreciate the thought of holding it in a mundane family restaurant. But neither Mike nor I had much money, and the offer, as this other couple's had been, was extremely good. So we accepted. I insisted, however, on supervising the arrangements myself. I might not like the casing but I could at least be sure of the insides.

On the morning of our wedding, October 26, 1974, I lay in bed just staring at my gown. It hung from a hook on my closet door, and its immaculate chiffon and twelve-foot veil made my white door and walls look drab. It had been delivered only the night before—three weeks since my fitting—but the wait had been worth it. I kept blinking my eyes, still refusing to believe. Was I really getting married?

Outside the church, I stepped from a gleaming black limo as a rugged wind slapped at my veil. The red blades of a windmill across the way twirled furiously, as a contingent of small black nuns struggled with their own veils near a stone convent at the side of the church. I looked at my father, his face stern, all emotion banked up behind his eyes. He was trying not to cry, and I knew he wouldn't. I looked at Carmen, my maid-of-honor. For a moment, we both locked each other's gaze, and everything, even the wild winds around us, stopped completely. "It's over," she said. "From now on, it's all new."

"Goodbye, my friend," my eyes replied. I felt a flood of tears I couldn't hold back. We embraced. I started inside.

I couldn't see a thing once I got in there. There were gracious guests on both sides of the aisles, but I just couldn't see them. Ballplayers, Kansans, Quebecois. I saw only one thing, a target at the end of a very long red carpet: a tall handsome man in an exquisite black velvet suit. I walked slowly toward him as the organ began to play. But as I moved down the aisle, I became overcome with doubt. Was I doing the right thing? Could I love him, would he love me back? If his pitching arm gave out, what would he do for work? Were my career and his compatible? Could this really work out?

At the end of the aisle, near the altar, I knew the answers. This church was a replica of Notre Dame with colossal stained glass windows, smooth marble statues, and an altar of thousands of carved gold leaves. The wedding's accessories were all in white: high candles, bushels of roses, streaming shiny ribbons. Even so, amid all this beauty, I saw only Mike. When I reached the altar, he looked at me and flashed that fabulous boyish grin. He placed his warm hand in mine and squeezed.

The ceremony began, and I thought: I'll never let go.

Our reception afterward was terrific. The arrangements Mike and I had made worked beautifully: five mariachi bands; a dinner of prime roast beef; lots of wine, champagne, and caviar; and little baby's breath centerpieces for all the tables.

Even the restaurant itself, when all was said and done, had become elegant. It had a little room downstairs called "The Sports Room." There we held a cocktail hour. On one wall was nothing but black-and-white glossies of local sports heroes, and on another were rows of baseball caps and soccer shirts. There was also a glass case of trophies, many won by athletic stars who patronized the restaurant's bar. The entire room was the perfect final touch.

After a wonderful honeymoon in Acapulco, we came to rest in a luxurious high-rise apartment in Montreal to begin our new life. I was Mrs. Torrez now, and I wondered what I could do to make our marriage an enviable success. One morning, early in December—just three weeks after our return from Mexico—I lay in bed staring at the big cardboard boxes, still unpacked, scattered around the room. Mike was beside me in our new king-sized bed, the biggest we could find. I looked at him sleeping soundly, his rumpled hair falling over his face, his left side against the sheet. I'd learned by now he never slept on his right: that big special right arm of his was our bread and butter.

I lay there and thought: what could I do to make this new home cozy, our own little nest? Potted plants, new carpeting, drapes. Furniture for the den. There was a lot to do. Our new life together in Montreal. Mr. and Mrs. Torrez. I'd model every afternoon and cheer wildly from the stands at night.

Suddenly, the phone rang. Mike woke at once and looked at me, still half asleep. Then it rang again. We both looked at the clock: 7:30. Mike frowned, picked up the receiver.

"Hullo?" he said, kind of groaning. Then he bolted straight up in the bed. "Oh, hello!" he said. His voice rose and his fingers started running through his hair. It was like he was combing it quickly for an unexpected guest.

61

Suddenly, his face turned gray. I'll never forget the color. Then he grabbed me by the arm, and his body sank slowly downward. He held the receiver away so I could hear. It was Jim Fanning, the Expos' general manager.

"You know, we really like you, Mike," Fanning was saying, "and we think you've done a great job for us. But, well, you know baseball."

I wasn't sure what that meant. But slowly I watched little tears form at the corners of Mike's eyes.

"Uh, do I call them, or do they call me?" he asked. "Oh, all taken care of, huh?" Suddenly, I knew what was happening: he was being traded! With absolutely no warning of any kind, the Expos were saying: you can't work here anymore, you can't even live here. Pack up, son. We're shipping you—and your wife—away.

"Is anyone going with me?" Mike asked. I heard his voice crack. "Oh, Kenny, huh?"

When he said that, I panicked: they're trading all the players who've married Canadian girls!

Mike said goodbye and hung up. He pulled me to his chest but didn't speak. I felt frightened: where were we going? And why? I thought of the business deals behind all this, maybe a luncheon in some exclusive downtown restaurant. Coaches, managers, owners getting together over cracked crabs and salad. "We could trade Torrez," one must have said. "I wonder where," would muse another. Our life transformed over some stranger's dessert or third martini. I looked up at Mike. For the first time since we'd met, he was crying. His pride was hurt. They didn't believe in him anymore . . . yet he had worked so hard.

I put my head back down on his chest and held him tight. I heard a train whistle by in the yard out back. And I thought, at least I'll have Colette.

TWO
BALTIMORE

Just three months after our honeymoon, I was back among the palm trees, this time in Florida for Mike's spring training with our new team, the Baltimore Orioles. I worried at first about the changes: my first time living outside Montreal, my first time in an English-speaking country—and Mike's first time in the American League. But I was determined to make the adjustment and to be a perfect baseball wife.

Surprisingly, the new league worried me more than anything. I had spent the last two summers learning baseball and getting familiar with National League rules, players, and statistics. Now, in one sudden swoop, I was starting from scratch.

"The American League's not really that different," Mike said. "About the only thing new is I won't have to bat." Unlike the National League, the American League permitted teams to add a tenth player, a designated hitter, who could bat instead of the pitcher throughout the game. To Mike, such a change was heaven-sent: like most pitchers, he was terrible

63

at the plate and hated going there. In his four years at Montreal, he'd averaged .154, and in baseball below .250 is considered not so good. In fact, the season before, Mike had reached his limit: he stood at the plate one day, straight up, no crouch or ready batting stance, and grinned maniacally at the opposing pitcher, the bat resting nonchalantly on his shoulder. As the ball came his way, he swung out with one hand, lunging wildly at a pitch too far away. Two lunges later, he was out. It was comic relief for a game that had already been won, and everyone in the dugout cracked up. When he tried harder, they knew, the result was usually the same.

Even if the new league's rules proved no problem, at least I could be thankful that the Orioles would never play Montreal. How could I cheer so hard for two years in my hometown, then abruptly switch loyalties and "love" a new team? At least being in a different league spared me that dilemma. Then I thought: what if Montreal and Baltimore faced each other in the World Series? But no, that was unthinkable: Montreal had never finished above fourth place, the Expos were still a young club with any real chance at a pennant far in the future. Baltimore, on the other hand, was already a winner!

Between 1969 and 1974, Manager Earl Weaver had built the Orioles into perennial contenders. They had won five division pennants and had played in three World Series. Their lineup included pitchers Jim Palmer and Mike Cuellar, both winners of the Cy Young Award, as well as a legend named Brooks Robinson, the best third baseman, many fans claimed in the history of the game. In the Eastern Division of the American League, every team feared and respected the Orioles.

Much of the reason for this was the leadership of Weaver himself. Mike knew of Earl Weaver even before he joined the Orioles, and he liked him a lot. "He always sticks up for hi

64

players," he once told me. But not until I saw this pudgy, energetic man in action could I truly understand what this meant.

If something went wrong, Earl Weaver believed, you corrected it on the spot. This attitude frequently caused him to do something baseball frowns upon—seriously question authority. Weaver was constantly challenging the highest authorities on the field, the umpires. You'd see him madly waving his arms or kicking dirt or stomping around on the mound. Once he went so far out of control, he actually tore pages from a rule book and hurled them at all four umps. When it came to challenging authority, Earl Weaver developed a reputation for having no equal.

When Weaver believed he was right, nothing could calm him. One year, during the final days of a pennant race, a game with Toronto was being played in pouring rain. Earl got very upset at this, but even more so because the Blue Jays' management refused to remove a heavy tarpaulin along the first base line. Afraid one of his players might trip and get hurt, he told the umps, "The rule book says 'no obstructions on the field or along the foul lines.' That tarp's gotta go."

The head umpire looked at him. "What if it doesn't?"

Weaver glared. "I'll pull all my players off the field," he said.

The umpire looked at him just as stern. "You pull your players off the field and you'll forfeit the game!"

An inning later, the tarp had still not been removed. Weaver began gesturing toward his players to come back to the dugout.

"Come on in," he yelled. "Come on."

Each player kind of looked around at the others, uncertain what to do. "Come on," Weaver yelled again, louder. "We're throwin' it in!"

The players began trotting to the dugout, and Weaver directed them inside to the clubhouse. The Orioles needed badly to win every game (it was late September), but Weaver held to his beliefs: it was dangerous out there, and the rules said "no obstructions." He would forfeit the game.

Other stories I heard about Weaver went even further than this. Once he argued vociferously with an umpire's call after a game had officially ended. His argument was that one of the rules had been ignored, allowing a run to score, and defeating the Orioles.

"You gave that runner too many bases," Weaver yelled at the umpires. "The run doesn't count."

By this time, the fans had gone, the broadcasters had closed up shop, and only the umpires and some of the players remained. But Earl kept insisting. Incredibly, though the game had been officially declared over, the umpires gave in. They brought the score back to a tie and resumed play. The result was that three more innings were played, with only a few members of the press still present and very few fans. But the Orioles won!

Being a member of a club with this kind of leader was, for Mike, a dream come true. Mike's manager in Montreal had been Gene Mauch. Mike had respected Mauch's baseball judgment, but was hampered by the fact that Mauch never really liked him. Mauch rarely stuck up for Mike and, for a while, even benched him. Mauch seemed to feel Mike was inadequate as a pitcher and didn't want to use him more than necessary.

Also, Mauch lacked a quality that Weaver possessed in abundance: the ability to develop his team's pitching. Mauch was one of those managers who paid more attention to offense than defense. But many veteran hurlers over the years looked back to their first years under Weaver as the best in their careers. This was true of Mike Cuellar, Steve Stone, Pat Dobson, and Rudy May. Mike looked forward to this opportunity as well.

With a club like Baltimore, competition to make the team could be fierce. Mike, however, was secure. In a trade that greatly pleased many Baltimore fans, Mike was replacing another pitcher, Dave McNally. Kenny Singleton had come over in exchange for outfielder Rich Coggins. While Mike and McNally had almost identical statistics from the previous year (both had fairly good earned run averages of 3.58), McNally was nearing the end of his career while Mike was approaching his prime. Kenny, too, had a decided edge on Coggins: both were .300 hitters, but Kenny could belt home runs and Coggins had a well-publicized sore arm.

"We'll trade with Montreal anytime!" was the feeling of many fans. If they performed in spring training as they had during the season, Mike and Kenny were assured jobs on opening day.

Mike and Kenny's security allowed the four of us—Colette and Kenny, Mike and I—to spend most of spring training having fun. We rented a large three-bedroom house together on Key Biscayne, with a beautiful garden, a living room that opened out into the breezy Florida air, and a swimming pool. One morning, I was standing in my white lacy house dress, just gazing at the pool's surface, when suddenly somebody's huge hand grabbed my waist, then a second hand gripped my left leg, and my feet lifted completely off the ground, up in the air, way up, and I grasped frantically at a mass of wavy black hair, but I couldn't hold on, and—poooosh!—I was in the pool! When I struggled to the surface, Mike, Kenny, and Colette were doubled over with laughter, standing between the pool and the living room, very dry.

"Mornin', hon," Mike called, still chuckling as he bent over to help me out. "Just a little joke." As I took his hand, though, I caught mischief in Kenny's brown eyes, and I pulled while he shoved from behind, and Mike sailed off the marble ledge, tumbling headfirst to join me in the water.

We enjoyed silly moments at the practice games, too, and tender ones. Once Colette and I sat high up in the stands watching Mike and Kenny sauntering along the first base line, and we began hooting and whistling, me with my arms flapping like a weird goose and Colette, more reserved, very elegantly lilting her palm. Our husbands responded heartily, Kenny grinning and gently tipping his hat, Mike tracing an imaginary heart in the air, with "I love you" forming sweetly on his lips.

Getting to know Colette was fun. I marveled at the huge breakfasts she'd prepare—ham, eggs, juice, potatoes, the works. I envied her steady decorum, hair precisely in place, always just the right level of makeup, and up-to-date fashions from Europe, Montreal, or the U.S. To me, Colette was a wonder. I was the little teen celebrity from Montreal, but Colette had been a model there, too, and much more: a manicurist and cosmetician, an airline stewardess, and a contestant in three Canadian beauty pageants. To me, these were tremendous accomplishments. Until now, I'd hardly been outside my hometown.

As time went on, I'd consider Colette even more exceptional, especially in the baseball world. She seemed so glamorous, even by the pool in her bikini and high heels. Her appearance challenged the demure and mundane look of the majority of players' wives. I began then to realize the players hoarded flashiness for themselves. They cast a glittering image for the fans and press, while at home they demanded dependable, practical, even boring wives. At all costs nonthreatening. Colette's style broke this cardinal rule. Fortunately, Kenny, from what I could tell, didn't mind a bit.

Her marriage to this tall, handsome black man also intrigued me. Montreal had few blacks, so I never gave much thought to prejudice. I did expect great troubles, though, as we moved south. But the whole time in Florida, no one in baseball commented on Colette and Kenny's mixed marriage even once: no player, coach, wife, or fan. It was as if no one dared put their opinions—positive or negative—into words. The matter just hung in the air. I realized the lengths to which a team would go to contain dissension. Don't make an issue of things, keep them to yourself. Play baseball.

Colette was not the only player's wife I got to observe closely during spring training. At an exhibition game in March at Miami Stadium, I grew to know two more. The first was Liz Mitchell, rookie pitcher Paul Mitchell's wife, who I watched fidgeting nervously in a seat one row ahead. With her white shorts and light blue halter, she looked like a schoolgirl, but I'd recognized her immediately, though I couldn't recall where we'd first met.

During the second inning, she turned and recognized me, too. "Nice to see you again!" she said, squinting through large, pink lenses. "You know, I've still got some extra pictures of the whales. Would you like a couple?"

The whales? Of course, the whales! This was Liz Mitchell, the wife of Paul Mitchell, a Baltimore rookie. We'd met them at Sea World just a few days before.

"I'd like that very much," I smiled as she twisted back to dig in her bag. Suddenly, an opposing batter cracked a hit, and we all jumped up to see where it went. Liz, balancing a hot dog and Coke in one hand and rummaging for the photo with the other, craned her neck toward the bullpen, toward Paul.

"I hope they put him in," she said, biting her lip and handing me the snapshots. Then she turned back, edged anxiously toward the front of her seat, and began blowing huge pink bubbles with her gum.

I wondered out loud why Liz seemed so nervous. "I guess a rookie in spring training is just like the other tryouts," I said to Colette. "He hasn't made it yet, he's probably still proving himself." Colette replied, "I'm glad Kenny and Mike don't have to go through all that. And us, too." Then we spotted another woman, who sat calmly with two boys. She was Dee Belanger, a veteran's wife. Though she was only about twenty-five, she seemed much older, not matronly, but more mature, settled. Where Liz was tense and edgy, Mrs. Belanger seemed almost too relaxed. She did, however, resemble Liz in many ways: they were both short and trim, used very little makeup, and had long straight blond hair. But Dee's husband, Mark, was an established player—he'd been a solid starting shortstop for Baltimore for several years—and she could afford the luxury of nonchalance. She chatted quietly with her sons and casually surveyed the crowd and the game. Only occasionally did she mark a play in her scorebook. Her husband would survive the cutoff, the odds were with him, though the nervous young woman in front of me couldn't yet be certain her own husband would, too.

"Dee's the woman I want to be," I thought. "She's done the job. She's made it."

I looked at her two young boys, about six and seven years old. I wanted desperately at that moment to unlock her secret. How had she supported her husband and his career and a family as well? I was frightened a little at such multiple responsibility, but I was sure I could succeed. I did wonder, however, where to begin.

The answer arrived on opening day. After Jarry Park, Baltimore's Memorial Stadium was somewhat intimidating, with its long, spooky corridors, grungy cement walls, and glaring exposed lights. People were running, shoving, bellowing at concession stands, on ramps, and in aisles on the levels above. The food alone could have fed Montreal: while Jarry Park had served the basics—hot dogs, burgers, french fries, and Cokes—here I found pizza, tacos, fried fish, beer, cotton candy, and chili! But most frightening of all, everything was in English!

I headed in the general direction of the wives' section, but wondered what would happen if I got lost and ended up somewhere embarrassing—like the visitors' locker room. I finally came up from the darkness, to a sunny aisle in the grandstands near the protective screen behind home plate. Immediately, I saw the familiar face of Dee Belanger, who was chatting with an usher.

"You made it!" she said. "Your first game in Baltimore!" She led me up more stairs, and I looked down at my ticket stub as we climbed: my first game in Baltimore, my first official game as Mike's wife. I would cherish this ticket forever!

"The wives' section," Dee pointed, after we'd reached some seats high in the rafters. I looked out and saw a horde of babies. I hadn't really noticed them back in Florida—perhaps their mothers had kept them at home then, away from the blazing sun—but at this moment, in the cool April of opening day, they'd all come out. There were babies scarcely two weeks old, their mothers clutching a scorecard in one hand and Pampers in the other; and there were kids a year or two older toddling across the aisle. It was as if the veterans, many with teenage sons and daughters, would very soon be gone, and it was time now to grow a new crop.

But that was what opening day was all about, and it was only one of the many unwritten "rules" I'd soon learn: as a baseball wife, your entire life focused on this day and the 161 other days like it throughout the year. Unless hospitalized or blocked by some other tragedy, you always came out to cheer. You went to every home game and followed, by radio or TV, every game on the road. Since your man's performance was continually measured and reported in the minutest detail by consumers (fans), employers (owners and managers), and outside analysts (the press), you were expected to counter this pressure with visible and enthusiastic support. Attending that initial game when all the heat began was a must.

"You should meet some of the girls," Dee said and pointed to various women: "Mary Garland, Jeanine Duncan, Byrd Grimsley, Marty Grich . . ." Some of them I already knew, like Brenda "Byrd" Grimsley who had welcomed me by telephone just after Mike's trade. Others I'd met in spring training. Most, though, were new, particularly the superstars' wives who had not been so visible back in Florida. Many last names were quite famous, and others I'd learned from conversations with Mike. When he'd spoken of them, they'd seemed foreboding.

"Jim Palmer's probably the best," Mike said once. "He's had four twenty-game seasons, a no-hitter, and his strike-out totals are outstanding. Not many pitchers can come close." I'd heard good things, too, of Brooks Robinson and his vacuum-cleaner fingers, of former Dodger batting whiz Tommy Davis, and of dazzling Cuban lefthander Mike Cuellar.

Now I was sitting among their wives. Surprisingly, they seemed much more down-to-earth than I could ever have imagined. Brooks' wife, Connie, was very attractive, in her mid-thirties, and stylishly dressed, and Jim Palmer's wife Susan also dressed well. But both were modest, clean-cut, even restrained. There was nothing extravagant or larger-than-life about them. Their behavior reminded me of Dee: they chatted pleasantly and smiled but seemed somehow aloof from the game itself. It occurred to me then that being the wife of a superstar was in many ways like being the wife of a politician: you lived every second in your husband's shadow. As the year went on, Susan Palmer would strike me as most chained by this role, faultless in dress and manners, always by Jim's side at banquets, parades, presentations. This bothered me at first, but later I began to admire her. I, too, after all, wanted to help my husband with his career and to be by his side. Susan was doing exactly that. It may even have been tearing her apart to be Jim Palmer's wife and little more, but she pressed forward and did it. I admired her for that, her determination. It was a life she chose and had made work.

I took my seat, deciding that if a veteran's wife did anything, it was to stay in the background and never display rampant energy. Later, however, during the seventh-inning stretch, Dee Belanger jumped up excitedly and began to bounce. "I love this song!" she exclaimed and jiggled back and forth as the current John Denver hit came pounding over the park's speakers.

Dee sang along with the lyrics, something about country boys and fine wives and funny riddles. She began snapping her fingers, too, and even the players down on the field got into the act. They interrupted their warm-ups by strumming bats and gloves like banjos and homemade guitars. I wondered then how far I'd really come: blaring American pop recordings versus the quaint little organ at Jarry Park and the rows of Expos fans resounding in chorus to a traditional "*val-da-ree, val-da-rah.*" But this was America, after all, and if a staid veteran's wife like Dee Belanger wanted to dance to John Denver, who was I to disapprove?

At one point during the game, I peered through my binoculars to look for Mike. I spotted him in the dugout, strutting, grinning, and chewing sunflower seeds. He turned casually, looking my way, his big brown eyes locked with mine, his smile steady as he ground away at the seeds. The little scar over his right eye arched noticeably, and he raised a thick index finger and moved it cooly up and down. I threw him a big wave in return but kept staring through the binoculars at his hat. On its front was the Orioles' insignia, a black-and-orange cartoon bird wearing a similar cap of its own. Mike had come here to pitch for the greater glory of that bird, and I shuddered, wondering how well I would help. Three games later I found out.

It had been Mike's first turn to pitch—starters usually work one day, then take three or four off for rest. A fan, very big and loud, had been heckling him all day.

"Hey, Torrez, go back to Canada!" he yelled, chugging beer after beer and getting harsher with every one. I had been surprised all week at the number of critical fans. In Florida, everyone had been so friendly, as if players and wives were long-lost cousins finally come home for a much-awaited family reunion. But in Baltimore, many fans were mean, crabbing at Mike even as he warmed up near the stands.

"Your fastball stinks, Torrez; throw sliders!" yelled a drunk hanging over the edge of his front row box seat. Mike, just a few feet away, ignored him completely.

"Sliders, Torrez, listen to me: forget your fastball, it doesn't work. *Sliders!!*" I was amazed at the man's arrogance. He didn't even know Mike, yet here he was, almost touching him, nearly screaming in his ear.

Now, another man was screaming in *my* ear, and worse, screaming as if he knew I was Mike's wife.

"C'mon, Torrez, ya bum; hang up your glove; get outta Baltimore!!"

His bellowing ran through me like ice. What did he know about baseball? Didn't he realize Mike was just recovering from a bad cold? That's my husband out there, I kept thinking, the man I love, he's doing the best he can, stop razzing him. What happens on that field affects both our lives, our future together, our hopes and dreams. How can a perfect stranger so easily dismiss us with "Go home, Torrez," or "Get outta town?"

74

I wanted to spin around and shut him up, but Colette said no. "He's just trying to get to Mike through you," she said. "Forget him."

He bellowed again, louder than before. I couldn't stand it. I frowned, leaned forward rigidly, trying to concentrate on the game and block him out. Colette grabbed my arm, holding it very tight. Without words, she seemed to be saying: "I'm warning you: You mustn't react. Don't even look at him. Don't do anything at all."

"You're nothin', Torrez," the man yelled then, "you really suck. Get off the field, willya? Go back to the farm!"

Three innings more of this and I began to feel very sick. I thought I might escape to the ladies' room or even leave the game altogether and go home. Before I could do either, I felt a cool trickle on the top of my head, then a slow wash down my neck. I realized in horror the man was pouring his beer all over me.

I couldn't have felt more crushed. My eyes filled up, the ballfield blurry through my tears. I turned back and finally looked at this cruel man, too hurt, and scared, to say a word.

"Sorry," he glared, his eyes shabby and cold. "It slipped."

I turned back and resolved to do as Colette had said. A player's wife must never react to what fans do because it's they who pay the freight. This newest rule was quite a test. I got up and walked to the ladies' room feeling ashamed and humiliated as the beer dribbled down my back and ruined my white coat and dress.

From what I'd heard from other wives, relations with fans had changed a lot since the well-mannered years of the fifties and earlier. I'd always heard stories of fans spontaneously buying dinner for players and wives after a game or sending birthday cards to a player's house or even dropping by for a friendly chat. Now it seemed that far too many fans had lost

75

control. The cute lovable ravings of the old Dodger rowdies at homey Ebbets Field had been replaced by a frighteningly hostile atmosphere. In Chicago's Comiskey Park, for example, if a wife wanted to go to the bathroom, it was necessary to take a male escort along to wait outside no more than five minutes before coming in after her! In other parks, like Chicago's Wrigley Field and Detroit's Tiger Stadium, and to a lesser degree all the others, tales of jostlings and even muggings and rapes were becoming much too common.

Even so, most players felt their wives represented them off the field. The rule—"never react"—was strictly obeyed. "If I ever catch you saying anything to a fan," one player put it, "I'll send you home. The fans pay my salary." So we absorbed taunts or tried to ignore them and held on, whenever possible, to our pride. I did hear of the occasional wife who argued back or called an usher or told a fan off. And very rarely, a wife would actually slug it out with a fan. At a game in Kansas City, a third baseman's wife even refunded a fan's admission!

"I laid out seven dollars for this seat," the guy bellowed at her. "I can say any damn thing I want."

The wife whipped out her checkbook and wrote the guy a check on the spot. "Here's your lousy seven bucks," she screamed, tearing out the check and flinging it at him, "Now get the hell out!"

The mania with which many fans approached this game truly took me by surprise. I began to learn that, on the East Coast in particular, in the oldest baseball cities, fans adored baseball with more intensity than I'd seen in Montreal. They brought gloves to catch foul balls and seat cushions to endure the later innings. Some fans kept records of the team's performance game-by-game, attended games on the road, or huddled in the stands with radios and even TVs to follow the commentary and play-by-play. Fans also wore clothing with

Orioles insignias, like hats, T-shirts, and running shorts. For the truly fanatic, the souvenir shop even sold Orioles underwear!

In Oakland, a wife spotted one of the team's catchers in a box seat sitting among the fans and quietly watching the game in full gear with his wire mask, big stuffed chest protector, well-worn catcher's mitt, and gritty spiked shoes. She asked a companion what he was doing there.

"Haven't you noticed him before?" came the reply. "He's there every game, he's not on the team at all! He's a season ticket holder!"

Sometimes, an individual would come forward and defend us from belligerent fans. A retired gentleman who attended all the games once set himself up as a kind of wives' "godfather," sitting with us and trying to protect us. Fights often started that way, a kindly fan sticking up for us, or for our husbands, as some loudmouth hurled one too many insults. In restaurants, too, fans complimented or consoled us or simply requested an autograph. Here, I became very adept at smiling genially at strangers, my mouth full of mashed potatoes and peas.

Much of this media fame scared me, though. I'd seen all this dazzle and illusion before while working in TV in Montreal. People are not better than everyone else simply because they're well known. Baseball nurtured this impression, as I had seen by my own reaction to the superstars' wives. But thankfully I recognized a significant twist.

As with all sports, fame in baseball could usually be equated with excellence and skill. Willie Mays, Joe DiMaggio, Mickey Mantle, Pete Rose: even nonbaseball fans knew these names. But how often had players become well known without similarly superb careers?

These thoughts made me glad for Mike. His rising fame had begun to protect him from more everyday troubles and insecurities. The high he felt, I felt, too. Other wives agreed: I'm special because my husband is special; it weds me to this game.

Still at least one wife in Baltimore confided a frightening sidelight. Though a superstar family, Brooks and Connie Robinson had maintained the same residence on the same suburban Maryland street for most of their married life. Everyone knew where they lived and occasionally an adoring fan would brazenly knock on their front door to ask for an autograph or just a glimpse of the man himself. With three sons and a daughter all under age ten, such easy access worried Connie, especially during road trips. She even called the police one day when she saw a stranger in a beat-up black car talking to her children in front of their school. Fortunately, the man turned out to be a well-meaning fan, not a kidnapper, but Connie's anxieties continued until the boys had fully grown.

"I used to double-lock my doors at night," she said. "I'd sleep in the same bedroom with all four children when they were very young. Everyone knew where we lived, and I just couldn't escape this terrible, gripping fear."

In my mind, probably the most sterling example of learning to accept life with the fans will always be Deborah Coleman, wife of Tigers' pitcher Joe Coleman. In 1975 he was having the worst year of his career. Deborah sat in the stands one day, keeping score to still another heartbreaking performance, and blocking out, when she could, abuse from the fans. Finally, as her husband got tagged for more runs, in the bottom of the fourth, Deborah snapped shut her book and listlessly looked down at the mound. She neither cried nor made excuses, simply sighed loudly, and murmured, "Oh, Joe, you're making an old woman of me."

But it wasn't Joe, she knew, who was giving her early wrinkles and gray hair. It was the fans.

*   *   *

A second rule I learned in Baltimore involved luck and chance. I once heard a classic baseball story about Babe Ruth who decided one day to hit a home run for a little boy in a hospital. Standing at the plate, he pointed his bat toward center field in Yankee Stadium and announced, "I'm hitting it out, right over there—for the kid!" He swung smoothly and confidently at the next pitch, whacking it, as he'd said, clear over the wall. It was a unique moment. But even a superhero like Babe Ruth could not routinely predict his performance. The best batters go into periodic slumps, just as the worst pitchers sometimes toss no-hitters. Why this is no one can explain. As a result, even those with the most consistent skills often pay homage to the odds and to superstition.

Mike, like many players, tied some superstitions to the behavior of his wife. He'd watch me closely whenever he pitched, and if I deviated from any habit, he let me know.

"You pitched well those last three innings," I said after a game in June.

"Yeah, I started feeling better around the seventh," he said. "Say, you got up about that time and went somewhere. Where did you go?"

"To get a hamburger," I said. "I was getting tired of always ordering hot dogs."

"How was it?" he asked.

"Terrible," I grimaced. "Too greasy, and it wasn't really cooked."

"Well, forget how it tasted," he snapped. "From now on, eat *only* hamburgers. It changed my luck." This, then introduced me to the second rule: support your husband's superstitions, whether you believe them or not. I joined players' wives who ate ice cream in the sixth inning or tacos in the fifth, or who attended games in a pink sweater, a tan scarf, or a floppy hat.

Probably the most insidious superstition I'd ever seen involved Jim and Susan Palmer. Jim Palmer was one player who possibly needed superstitions the least. For one thing, he drank neither alcohol nor soda. He'd heard that sugar in soda caused tendonitis, so he refused to indulge. In fact, he so protected his health he used to feud about it constantly with Earl Weaver.

"I have more fights with Jim Palmer than with my wife," Weaver once said. "The Chinese tell time by the 'Year of the Horse' or the 'Year of the Dragon.' I tell time by the 'Year of the Back,' the 'Year of the Elbow.' Every time Palmer reads about a new ailment, he seems to get it. This year it's the 'Year of the Ulnar Nerve.'"

Weaver went on. "Someone once asked me if I had any physical incapacities of my own. Know what I answered? 'Sure I do,' I said. 'One big one: Jim Palmer.'"

Palmer, though, had also a superb eye for the game itself. What's more, he was not afraid to display it. He once walked off the field and gazed from the foul line into the outfield. He was like a painter sizing up a landscape. There were two outs, but he waved his leftfielder way over to the right, and in. He had an idea, he thought, that his next pitch would be hit right there. Such an action should have labeled him a prima donna. But on the very next pitch, the batter swung and smashed a hard line drive to precisely where Palmer had predicted. The inning was over.

When something goes wrong, Palmer gets very upset. I once saw him smash his glove to the ground when an outfielder dropped a routine fly ball. Another time, he turned and glared at new shortstop Doug DeCinces, who let a ground ball go through his legs. Palmer, if he thought anyone or anything was causing him to lose, could be merciless in his reactions.

Superstitions, then, to Jim Palmer, were as worthy of consideration as anything else. If luck was something he could use to his advantage, he would not ignore it. While Susan was vacationing in Greece, Jim had won a superb five straight games. The day she returned, however, he got bombed in the first inning and lost.

"You jinxed me," he said after the game. "From now on, just watch me on TV." Until he relented, she was forced to do just that, "attend" games by watching them on the Advent TV at the Hit and Run Club, the ballpark's restaurant and wives' hangout.

For the most part, though, these superstitions were only harmless fun. Some of the guys would eat favorite foods before a game, like Mike's spaghetti or Palmer's stack of hotcakes. I once heard of a player on the Phillies who, just before every batting practice, devoured an entire stalk of raw broccoli.

There were also those who wore particular items, say a neck chain or a pair of lucky shoes. Mike once wore the same pair of yellow underbriefs for five starts. He'd won the first game while wearing them and decided to wear them again and again until he lost. This, of course, was the general reasoning behind players' superstitions: to repeat an action from a previous day when the player had had a good game. Milwaukee manager Harvey Kuenn has been known to wear the same jersey during a pennant drive or championship playoff. Mets' outfielder Rusty Staub uses the same batting gloves until he hits a slump; then he puts them away until the slump ends.

It was Paul Mitchell who took the clothing ritual about as far, I thought, as it could go. His habit was to dress himself from the right side: he'd pull on his right pant leg, then his right sock, then slip his pitching arm into his right sleeve, then put on and tie his right shoe. If he got a phone call at that moment, he'd be standing at the phone with his right side fully clothed and his left completely nude. If he had a bad game, he might drop the idea for a week or two. But if he picked it up again and a good performance followed, he'd always repeat it next game.

81

Other superstitions were priceless. Satchel Paige, the ageless star of the old Negro Leagues, used to rub snake oil on his pitching arm before every game. Giants' pitcher Ron Bryant used to sit in the dugout with a teddy bear.

Pete Rose, in his early days, always coated his bat with talcum powder so he could see how the ball marked it when he connected. These markings, he maintained, helped him analyze how solidly he'd hit the ball. Because of this, he claimed, his hitting steadily improved. As the years went by, however, he needed these calculations less and less. Nevertheless, he kept up the ritual. It had become his superstition and he now couldn't feel comfortable without it.

Other players did things like carving their initials into favorite bats, throwing sand over their left shoulders, or carrying lucky coins or rabbit's feet. "I'd try anything," one player admitted, "so I won't have to feel so alone out there."

The rituals could sometimes be annoying. Cleveland first baseman Mike Hargrove daily irritated thousands with his prebatting motions. He made ten very specific moves before each pitch: kicked the dirt, pulled at his batting gloves, adjusted his helmet with his left hand, tapped both shoes with his bat, swung the bat once with one hand, again with both hands, touched his back, right shoulder, and mouth, and finally swung the bat a third and final time with both hands. Impatient players in the other team's dugout often cried out in frustration with each swing: "There's one!" they'd chant. "Two!" "THREE!" And the lengthy procedure annoyed everyone else, too: media commentators, reporters, and fans who wrote letters demanding that he stop. But no matter how much pressure Hargrove received, he refused to stop. If he was at the plate, say, four times in a game and took twenty pitches, he'd go through the entire process all twenty times.

One year, even an owner got involved with superstitions. In 1976, the Orioles' Jerome Hoffberger hired an authentic African witch doctor to parade atop dugouts and put hexes on opposing teams. The doctor began his duties by traveling to Boston with the O's and waving his hands during a night game and bellowing incantations. The Sox lost.

The next night the Boston fans were ready. As the good doctor jumped up onto the visitors' dugout near third base, he was inundated by wreathes of garlic and nearly choked to death right there by the stands!

These incidents gave one of Boston's TV stations an idea. Though she knew nothing of baseball, as a publicity stunt, Laurie Cabot, a self-professed witch from Salem, Massachusetts, was asked to travel to Cleveland with the Red Sox and help them break a slump. Always eager for a new experience, Laurie agreed.

Players, however, were very confused. No one had explained to them why Laurie was there, or what she thought she could do. She padded around the Red Sox dugout in black robes and wearing a shiny gold amulet, until the Sox designated hitter, Bernie Carbo, asked: "Can you make my bat into a magic wand?"

Laurie replied, "What I can do is what I do. I can produce very strong alpha waves and put a shield around both you and the team. I can give the Red Sox a 'group aura.' You'd then all have 'like' energy. You'll be much more connected with each other than you've ever been before."

Carl Yastrzemski came up to her and said politely: "If you can do anything, please do it." The team had lost its last nine games. Yaz, like any smart veteran, was amenable to any solution.

Carlton Fisk, however, was not. "What's she doing here?" he screamed, then began stomping around the field. "Get her out of here! This is serious business. We don't need her here."

The game got underway, and Laurie sat with Len Berman, the TV announcer, in the broadcast booth. She went as far as she could go, announcing during the eighth inning that a very strong alpha shield was now in place. More important, it would remain there about four days. Then, she warned, the energy would dissipate and quickly wear away.

The Sox won the game that day, and, miraculously, the next three as well. On the fifth day, though, the Sox lost again. Then on the sixth and seventh, they plunged back into their slump. Laurie's alpha shield, apparently, had broken apart.

On-the-field superstitions were not the end of it, however: we wives developed rituals, too. An Oakland wife ironed during every road game; a Cincinnati wife washed her hair when her husband pitched. Ex–Pittsburgh outfielder Ralph Kiner's wife, Nancy, used to wear gold earrings with the number 4 on them to every game—same number as Ralph's uniform. My own superstition was my "lucky pen" which I always used for scoring. During that first game in Montreal, I'd kept score with a silver and light blue Papermate, which I used from then on. I held it a certain way, too, sticking my index fingers, when not writing, behind the clip. Once, at a game in July, I couldn't find the pen in my bag and refused a wife's offer of a substitute.

"Not a pen," I said. "Let me have one of your son's crayons." It was a thick, green Crayola, and it made ugly fat lines, but I used it anyway. Some other pen would've broken the luck.

The fun backfired when Mike Hargrove's wife, Sharon, wore her "lucky dress." While playing with the Texas Rangers, Mike's team had been having a rough time, losing game after game and floundering hopelessly in the cellar. One night, after losing several games in a row, by some miracle, they finally won. Sharon decided that her pretty yellow dress had produced the luck.

"I think I'll wear it every night till we lose," she announced flippantly to the other wives. She assumed that the Rangers' prowess would never last.

The next night, Texas won again, and the night after that! Soon, a week had gone by, and her fresh springtime chemise was covered with mustard stains, coffee spills, and streaks of perspiration.

"No, no, you can't wash it," the players said. "You'll wash the luck out. You've got to keep it on!"

Mercifully, two days later the team lost, but not before a photographer from the *Ft. Worth Star–Telegram* had captured her on film. In the photo, she looked both cute and miserable, her luck-wracked dress sallow and limp. Friends and fans surrounded her in the photo on all sides, holding their noses and leaning far, far away.

Conversation in the stands invoked a third rule: there were things you talked about and things you did not. Unfortunately, acceptable topics were very dull: children, vacation plans, parents, neighbors, your husband's sore knee or arm. Attempts at serious discussion, like politics or current events, were frowned upon as if they might detract from the all-important game.

We did talk about the game at times, but with a hitch: you were never to comment on a player's error. If Mike was pitching and Mark Belanger booted a double play, I'd say nothing to Dee. We all hated the way the fans jumped on our husbands, so we refused to spread hurt feelings among ourselves. We also admonished our guests to keep still. "The team is paying for these tickets," one wife explained. "If you call a player a 'bum,' his family might be sitting in the next row." And besides, I thought, a bum today could be a hero tomorrow. You never knew.

Even so, we couldn't help getting upset at times. Ultimately, we were not sitting here just for fun: errors and inept play meant smaller crowds, the loss of a pennant, less money. Outwardly, when a player screwed up, we'd appear noncommital. But if it happened too often, we'd boil with rage inside.

Salaries were never discussed for the same reasons. Resentment flowed easily in a sport where paychecks varied so widely. As recently as the decade before, salaries could go as low as $3,000 or $4,000 while superstars, like Boston's Ted Williams or Detroit's Al Kaline, were making thirty times more. Though the players' union, in 1975, had just negotiated a minimum salary of $28,000—in 1982, it had risen to $32,500—even so, the disparity continued and would get worse in 1976 with the free agent draft.

Problems had always been around because bonuses with players' initial contracts and the strength of their agents always made some players seem vastly overpaid. So, although we often had a rough idea from the sports pages what other husbands were making, the potential for dissension prohibited us from ever discussing the subject at all.

Another forbidden topic was players' girlfriends. Once I spotted an unfamiliar, pretty, young face, sitting alone a few rows back. I asked Colette who she was.

"Don't ask," Colette frowned, as if she knew, and I realized then why so many of the Montreal wives had at first resented me. Until it had become clear I was with Mike as a girlfriend, I'd been a frightening symbol. It was better that a wife not even ask than risk the revelation that the cute teenager in the back row was her own husband's "groupie."

So though my marriage was just six months old, I got my first taste of the possibilities that awaited it. Somehow this pretty groupie, only two or three years younger, made me feel very old. Would the day come when Mike might trade me in? I looked back toward the field. The other wives refused to acknowledge her and so would I. I had learned one more aspect of my role.

As the year went on, I became totally absorbed in Mike's career. It was being improved, I noticed, not only by the attention and support of Earl Weaver, but by others on the team as well. Brooks Robinson, for example, advised Mike one day to stop trying so hard for strikeouts.

"Force the batter to hit more grounders," he said. "You've got the backup, right?" With Robinson himself at third, Mark Belanger at short, Bobby Grich at second, and Lee May at first, Mike's answer was, "Yes, of course!"

As a result of such advice, by late August, Mike's earned run average hung steady at 3.00, a very good ratio. He was also heading, I calculated, for career highs in strikeouts, complete games and innings pitched. He had even tied a personal record for wins—the sixteen he'd garnered three years earlier in Montreal. So, as I turned on the TV to watch him step to mound in Minnesota for a try at seventeen, I knew how much it meant for him to win.

Starting pitchers pray each season for twenty wins. It's the standard by which leaders escape the pack. It means a shot at the record books, respect from almost every fan, and a tremendously strong bargaining chip when haggling with owners over next year's pay. Mike had come close to twenty wins twice before—a 16–12 season in '72 and a 15–8 season in '74—but this time his pace was right on track. If he won today, barring disaster in September, he'd make it.

If he did win today, we'd really celebrate. I checked my preparations. I'd cooked a gourmet meal for him, planned decorations, even ordered a specially made silver trophy just for the occasion.

Catcher Dave Duncan's wife, Jeanine, knocked softly on my

door and came inside. Her blue eyes widened as she looked at what I'd done. "Oh, D, this table looks so nice," she said, scrutinizing my dining area. Jeanine was a quiet, wonderful friend who joined me during road trips to watch the games. She always offered tactful optimism, but my apartment was the ultimate test: its furnishings, chosen by Mike, included an avocado green shag rug (with mustard-colored threads), a black, white, and orange striped sofa and chair, sickly mud-brown drapes, a chrome kitchen table, and black vinyl chairs. I hated the place, and Jeanine, as usual, tried to cheer me up.

Today, though, her task was a breeze. The dining table did look beautiful. There were black linen placemats, matching napkins, white sweetheart roses, sleek long-stemmed candles, and bone-colored octagonal plates. Underneath a small salad dish lay an envelope and personal note. "Missed you *mon petit lapin* (my little bunny)" I'd written. "Happy you're home— your wiff." He always called me that, his "wiff." Jeanine noticed the envelope but left it alone. It reeked of perfume and had a big smudge of lipstick for a seal. She smiled knowingly.

"Come help me color these pictures," I urged, and she joined me on the couch. I was preparing for Mike's return that night, hoping we'd have good reason to celebrate. I'd torn apart many children's coloring books to collect the right pictures—bears running and swinging sticks and throwing big balls—and now I was coloring them and scribbling teasing comments. Mike's size had earned him a nickname in Baltimore, "The Big Bear." I planned to greet him at the airport that night with the inside of our powder-blue Cadillac covered with these cutout bears, followed by a candlelight meal when he got home.

"This is so romantic," Jeanine said, sitting down and grabbing a crayon. Somehow, even my ugly furniture seemed nicer with Jeanine in the room. She always reminded me of a bright flower that had only fully bloomed the night before.

"I hope he wins this game," I said as we both looked at the screen. Jeanine's husband, Dave, was catching and he'd just come out to the mound, apparently to calm Mike down. As catcher, it was his job to help the Orioles' pitchers maintain their control. Mike, in particular, was notorious for losing his.

"Oh, Jeanine," I said. "Do you think a relief pitcher's warming up?"

"In the second inning, D? Don't worry about it." She'd been a baseball wife two years longer than I, so I trusted her judgment. "He's just finding his groove. He'll settle down."

And he did, too, until the fifth inning. The game was tied, 2–2. I crossed my legs for good luck as Mike walked one batter, then a second, then threw two balls for a 2-and-0 count to batter three. Jeanine and I stopped coloring and stared blankly at the set. The fifth inning was a crucial checkpoint for a starting pitcher because he could not officially chalk up the win unless he pitched it all the way through and his team had a lead and held it. As Mike blew a fastball by the batter for a called strike, then a slider, low and away, for ball three, I bit hard on my lower lip, scared.

"Oh, Jeanine, I hope he's not blowing it," I said as the manager, Earl Weaver, walked slowly to the mound. Hopefully, he was just checking with Mike to see how he felt: I knew he wouldn't leave Mike in if he thought he'd lost control. The camera zoomed in on Mike's face, showing a tense, pensive look as he stared down at the ground and turned the ball around and around by the seams. Please, God, I thought, let him stay in. Then Dave came out and joined them, but soon trotted back behind the plate, as Weaver patted Mike lightly on the rump and returned to the dugout.

Jeanine couldn't watch now and buried her head in her arms as I poured us both a glass of wine. The camera focused again on Mike's face. There was now one out, two men on base, and a count of 3 and 1. Mike shook away a sign, then shook again. His indecision was getting me anxious, but then he straightened up, glanced to first, raised both arms, swiveled his hips, and flung his right arm hard. The ball sailed with the surety of that first potato back in Kansas. Another slider, a swift, sharp curve down and outside. "Strike two," bawled the umpire. Full count, 3 and 2.

At that moment, I wondered how Mike felt. It would mean so much to him to win today, to prove something to his family back home and to his friends, teammates and proud young wife. The pure white of the ball marked sharply his fingers' dark brown skin. Would the prejudice he'd encountered all his life now retreat? Could a dirty Mexican measure up if he won twenty games? Perhaps now he'd see.

My legs were getting numb, but I couldn't uncross them and risk breaking the luck. "Make the batter swing," I said aloud. "Oh, please God, make him strike out."

Mike went through his routine again, the glance at first, the arms high, swivel, lean forward, and the ball jigged straight at the plate, a strike certainly, a perfect pitch. The batter swung away with all he had, swung swift and clean and connected, popping it up.

"Foul behind the screen at home," the TV announcer said dully. "Still 3 and 2."

A replay came on the screen—a replay? Come on, I thought, for a crummy foul?—and I considered divorcing him right there. How could I live with this tension? But as the umpire threw Mike a new ball, I changed my mind: I'll stay with you, babe, only strike the bum out! And hurry now, or I'll lose all circulation in my legs!

Mike's face once more flashed on the screen. He took a heavy, deep breath. Then he wound up again, cocked his arm way back and threw. The batter connected once more, but this time the ball skittered straight toward shortstop Mark Belanger, who scooped it cleanly off the ground and flipped it to second baseman Bobby Grich, who then flung it to Lee May at first, for a double play. The O's had done it! Mike had survived the fifth, could now officially record the win, and, after Baltimore having scored two more runs in the top of the seventh, he did! The camera caught him grinning from ear to ear as he strode off the field at the end of the game.

"Oh, my little friend," cried Jeanine, teary-eyed. "I'm so happy: his seventeenth win!"

Nervously, I looked at the clock. "He'll be at the airport before I know it," I said, and Jeanine hugged me, then quickly left. I turned on the stove and the oven. By the time I returned, dinner would be warmed and ready to go—salmon in cream sauce, quails with chicken broth and sautéed onions. I quickly stroked on my mascara and blush, then slipped into pants, a loose tunic, high heels, and the diamond-heart neck chain Mike'd given me for our wedding day. Would he appreciate the bears, I wondered? Or would he be too embarrassed in front of the guys? I'd park the car, I decided, in a remote area of the parking lot so his teammates wouldn't see. I left with the little trophy and Cordon Rouge in an ice bucket for the ride home.

An hour later, in the airport's long lobby, I stood far back and watched the crowd. The players were always greeted, after a successful road trip, by throngs of enthusiastic fans. I liked to lean against the wall near the Budget Rent-a-Car booth and survey each player as he came through. An outfielder, Don Baylor, emerged first, then pitcher Wayne Garland and Doug DeCinces, followed by Brooks Robinson, Bobby Grich, and another young pitcher, Doyle Alexander. I was fascinated, as usual, by how nonchalant they all acted, seemingly oblivious to the fans and press, so completely unlike the fashion hounds I'd known in Montreal. Pitcher Ross Grimsley went immediately to his wife Byrd and picked up their young son, gave Byrd a hearty kiss, then the three of them, and their dog Floozy, strolled away.

"Hey!" came a voice, as Mike threw his trench coat playfully over my head.

"You won!" I said, looking out from under the coat. "Number seventeen! You won, you won!!"

"Yeah," he said, grinning widely. "How 'bout that?"

"See what marriage does for you?" I said, as he tucked me under his arm. I felt suddenly protected, his arm like some angel's great golden wing.

"What did you think of that strikeout in the fourth?" he asked.

I looked at him in mock irritation. "You didn't strike anyone out in the fourth." He occasionally tried to trick me, to test how closely I'd watched the day's game or if I'd watched it at all. But I'd learned a lot in the past couple of years. "You walked two batters, though, I remember that. And two more in the fifth! Don't ever put me through that again. I almost divorced you!"

He smiled, shook his head, then put a hand to his right shoulder. "I was loose, though," he said, rubbing it. "God, was I loose!"

"Even with 138 pitches?" I said.

"Yeah, a bit much, I guess, huh? But even so I still felt good. I still can't believe it!"

We soon arrived at the parking area, and he looked out, confused. It was nearly empty.

"There weren't any spaces here before," I said innocently. "I parked around the corner."

"Come on," he said. "What did you do now?"

"Nothing," I lied. "I didn't want to dent our fender."

He shook his head again as I led him to the car. Then, when he saw it, with its "Welcome Home" banner and its orange and black streamers, he threw his head back and laughed as hard as he could.

"You're a crazy wiff," he said, "you know that? You're nuts."

We got inside and kissed. I handed him the champagne and he popped the cork, staring all the while at the colored bears on every side.

"What made you think of this?" he said. "What made you do this?" But I wouldn't answer him, just kept smiling and kissing him softly on the back of his neck. Then, I handed him a little rolled-up piece of paper, tied daintily with a bright orange ribbon. He unraveled it carefully, curiously, then his expression burst with delight.

"Your scorecard!" he cried. It was a permanent record of today's victory.

He raised his glass. "To a twenty game season," he said.

"Just three more wins," I toasted.

"That each homecoming will be as nice as this. That you never lose your craziness." Then we clinked our glasses, and he looked at me, very sure.

"To a baby," he smiled, and we kissed for a long time and hugged all the way home.

Both players and wives considered road trips the most arduous aspect of life in the major leagues. Ballplayers spend about half the season away from home, eighty to ninety games in all. Road trips last from three days to two weeks, and in each month there are at least two, sometimes three or four. Road trips were where the players did most of their fraternizing. During the season, pro ballplayers spent so much time at the park or on the road, there was little left over for anything but quiet time at home. Very rarely did they see each other anywhere else. Occasionally, Mike and I would join Dave and

Jeanine for dinner at a nice restaurant, or we'd go out with a few of the players and their wives after a game for a quick sandwich or pizza. But full-blown parties during the season, so far as we knew, were the exception, not the rule, as were gatherings of any sort.

During the off-season, it was even quieter. Everyone headed home to disparate parts of the continent. At our wedding, for example, we'd only had four ballplayers: Kenny Singleton, Ron Woods, Bill Stoneman, and Steve Rogers. All the rest lived hundreds or thousands of miles away. Consequently, the road trips were where the players got together for most of their "fun."

For the wives, road trips meant a considerable upset of our routines. This was true since, when the players were home, we wives structured our lives totally around them. We'd prepare big midday meals, endure long drives to the park, watch warm-ups, pregame shows, and the game itself. Worst of all, we'd wait for what seemed like days outside the locker room after every game. We might wait as much as ninety minutes or a couple of hours, sitting on long wooden benches in an adjoining corridor, our backs against a concrete wall. For an hour or so, I could stand it—mostly reading or talking with Jeanine or Colette—but during the second hour, I'd anxiously keep looking up at the door, praying that it would open and Mike would finally come out.

"Is he almost ready?" I'd ask Dave Duncan or Kenny Singleton.

"Oh, *your* husband said he'd be out in ten minutes," they'd say. Then, they'd motion to their wives, start off, and look back at me over a shoulder. "He's still blow-drying his hair."

But waiting was part of my job, so I didn't get angry. "I had to put some ice on my arm," Mike'd say, or, "Some reporter was chewin' off my ear." Then he'd tuck me under his arm and we'd head home. And I'd think, well, after all, it's how we pay the rent.

These huge chunks of time created black voids when the guys were on the road. Many of us lived at an apartment complex in a town called Cockeysville, some forty minutes outside Baltimore. We'd picked up leases from the pro football players and their wives who had left two months before. During road trips, we gathered at the swimming pool and did needlepoint, swapped recipes, read Gothic novels, discussed the soaps—and thought about our men. Occasionally, there'd be a party, though often they were cliquish affairs and I wouldn't be invited. Other than Colette and Jeanine, I really didn't fit in with most of the other wives. They seemed to group together by personality—Marty Grich and Mary Garland, for example, were fun-loving and liked to throw parties; or by status—I noticed Susan Palmer, Dee Belanger, and Connie Robinson often sat together at many games. But there was no strong attempt to make us all function together as a unit, so some of the wives spent these times completely alone, just minding their kids or watching TV. Since I already knew Colette, and since Jeanine was almost everyone's friend, I fell in easily with both of them. The rest of the time, however, I spent mainly gazing out the window, longing for Montreal.

Jeanine, who wrote poetry, once expressed the mood many of us felt as our husbands chased little white balls around the country, totally preoccupied with baseball and little else, while we all waited patiently back home:

> You come into my
> thoughts quite
> regularly and it
> is such a lonesome
> feeling . . .

because I am not
in your thoughts.

One wife complained about the lack of sex. "Sometimes you just want to make love to somebody," she said, "but there's no one around. There's always a dark moment when you go stumbling around the empty apartment, mumbling to yourself. It gets you crazy."

The feeling during road trips, then, was like living in limbo. We were single girls hauling trash or jousting with mechanics, and we were single-parent mothers caring for toddlers and growing teens. Since troubles might upset a player's game, many wives would refuse even to mention problems when their husband telephoned from the road. "There's nothing he can do anyway," they'd say. "I'll tell him when he gets back."

When he did return, however, everything changed. "I'm so glad you're here," many a wife would babble as her weary husband dragged himself through the door. "I've been cooped up with these kids ever since you left. Take over, let me go for a walk or something. I've just got to get out of here for a while."

But the husband often felt otherwise. "Hold on a minute," he'd snap. "I can't handle this just yet. I just got off the road. Let me relax a minute, OK?"

Most of us, though, were eager to build our lives around our husbands the moment they came home. We'd drop everything else for the next week or ten days, skipping classes if we took a course or taking time off from work, even abandoning neighbors and friends.

"When my husband's home, I want to be with him," one wife said, "not sitting around the kitchen table with someone else." Those who became friends understood this. Friendships flowed in shifts: when players were away, they flourished; when players came home, they all but ceased to exist.

Because of road trips, I also learned more about the activities of teenage groupies. I'd begun to see these groupies leaning over the dugout at the end of the games, wearing tight rock-and-roll T-shirts, cheap high heels, and faded skintight jeans. I learned that these girls made themselves readily available to the players during road trips. As a result, none of us could ever be really sure our own husband was not involved.

To live with this anxiety, some wives created distinctions. If a wife learned that her husband merely took a young female out to dinner, she might actually be relieved. Sex itself was the real worry, right? And most wives coped with that one by praying that, if anything did happen, they'd simply never find out about it.

Jeanine, however, once thought she did. She telephoned Dave at 3:00 A.M., and, receiving no answer, feared the worst. But Dave reassured her the next day that he'd simply been out with the guys. For the first couple of years of their marriage, she suffered constant anxiety over the possibility that some woman somewhere might find her husband irresistible, and he'd not push her away.

Rookie pitcher Mike Flanagan's wife, Kathy, saw the threat up close. While still engaged, just a few months before their marriage, she sat in the players' parking lot in a parked car and watched a Baltimore infielder wooing a buxom young girl with a scruffy backpack.

"But he's married!" she cried as the girl got into the player's car. To another wife in the car, she said: "Is this what goes on in the majors? If it is, I'm not sure I want to marry into it."

In dealing with this constant worry, an outfielder's wife one day took it upon herself to help us all. About ten of us, while waiting for our husbands after a game, were in a ladies' room when we witnessed two groupies grooming themselves and chatting by a sink.

"Do you think any of the players will come to our party tonight?" one groupie said.

"They've come before," said the other. "I'm sure they'll want to." The outfielder's wife, a large, almost muscular woman then moved between them, placing two ready fists on her hips.

"Listen, you two," she snarled. "I've seen you here before. In fact, don't I recall warning you to stay away from our husbands?"

One of them, however, just stuck out her Dolly Parton breasts and refused to budge. "It's a free country," she said, teasing a comb through her hair. "We're not afraid of you."

Suddenly, the wife swung out and cracked the girl in the jaw. The girl's blond head spun wildly as she careened off the sink and landed spread-eagled on the blue-and-white tiled floor.

"My father will sue," she sobbed. Her father was a prominent Baltimore lawyer.

"Aww, go ahead and sue, ya little tramp," growled the wife, as the rest of us began to applaud.

Fortunately, this anxiety only affected me indirectly, since I knew that Mike didn't cheat. "I'm 99.9% sure of it," I announced at lunch one day to the other wives. It was a huge surprise, then, when one of them pulled me aside.

"Don't be a fool," she said. "They all cheat, even my own husband. I've been really disgusted for a long time." She confided, "Just before we married, I was at his old apartment and saw a coffee cup and a cigarette butt, both with lipstick stains, beside his bed. He denied it, of course, said he'd lent the apartment to one of his friends, but I could tell he was lying. That's the part that bothers me most, the lies." She looked away, stared out the window for a minute, and sighed.

"I can tell it's still going on, too," she said slowly. "I see the little postcards with their 'I miss you' notes and strange women's signatures. I get wrong numbers much too often, little girls' voices that say, 'Oooo, sorry,' then hang up quick. I'm telling you, my man's just like all the others." Then she looked at me, sternly. "And that includes Mike!"

I literally froze when she said this, just couldn't believe her. I was trying my best to be a good wife, to be a love he couldn't dismiss. I thought we were pretty happy, at least I knew I was. Why would he possibly go off with someone else? Wasn't I enough for him?

I wanted to say, "I'm sorry your own marriage is disappointing, but why take it out on me? Mike doesn't cheat, he just wouldn't. He has no need."

After the last game of the season, though, I was no longer sure. Liz Mitchell and I were in that same ladies' room and two groupies were again grooming and chatting by the sink.

"It's the end of the year," one said. "Last chance to see the guys." She started naming some of the players she hoped would show up at a particular nightclub that night. Then she said, "Do you think Torrez'll be there, too?"

The other replied without skipping a beat, "Probably. He usually is, isn't he?"

I couldn't believe what I was hearing and once more couldn't even react.

Most often, Mike came straight home with me. But when I was not at the game, he sometimes went off with the guys "for a quick bite." Once in a great while these "quick bites" lasted till 3 or 4 A.M. But I'd always completely believed him.

There was no way, however, I could deny this one. It had truly slapped me across the face. Liz heard it, too, and only looked at me, saying nothing. We both hurried out.

"Oh, shit," I heard one of them say as we left. "That was his wife. Now, I'm sure he won't come."

THREE

OAKLAND

On my twenty-third birthday, April 2, 1976, Mike was traded to Oakland. The rival Boston Red Sox had edged out our Orioles, frustrating Earl Weaver's hopes for three straight pennants. Though second-place overall, the O's had finished next to last in extra-base hits. Apparently the Orioles' management decided they needed more power hitting for next year. Scanning the lists of batting leaders for 1975, they saw one name shining through: Oakland Athletics outfielder Reggie Jackson.

Reggie Jackson had been a star for a long time. He'd led the American League twice in home runs, he'd driven in over 100 runs a season three times, and, in 1969, he'd spent much of the year vying for Roger Maris's single-season record of 61 home runs. That year he'd actually ended far short of the mark with 47, but was still considered, then and now, one of the more unforgettable sluggers of modern baseball. When he swung hard at a pitch, you could practically hear the wind whistle all around him. A team that needed hitting could covet no one more.

To get Reggie, Baltimore gave up a lot. Mike's 20–9 record had led the league in winning percentage (.690). Oakland demanded him, hot young outfielder Don Baylor, and Liz Mitchell's husband, Paul. Paul had pitched part of the year in the minors, only joining the club in June. He had a great start though and quickly compiled a record of 3 and 0.

For Mike, this trade would move him up a notch: Oakland was even more a contender than Baltimore, having won three consecutive World Series, in '72, '73, and '74. When it came to wins and losses, Mike was like most of the other players. There were so many games each year, it was impossible to get too upset about any one of them. For the bigger games, though, like the playoffs or the World Series, emotions ran wild. In 1972, for example, when the Red Sox battled the Tigers right down to the last day of the season, I'd heard that Sox outfielder Carl Yastrzemski had cried openly near his locker after the loss. Someone saw him that day and said, "I bet if the Tigers had lost today, Al Kaline would be crying just as hard."

Mike wanted those kinds of experiences. He'd never been in the World Series or even the playoffs. He was thus elated to be welcomed as a worthy member of a team that routinely took part in them.

For me, the trade was a good thing, too. I abhorred Baltimore, with its desolate downtown and high crime. I always felt I saw panic on the faces of its people. The city's whole atmosphere seemed so old and crumbling.

San Francisco instead looked bright, alive, golden, and free. You could see nature there, and a vibrancy that reminded me of Montreal. It was progress, another step toward my dreams.

I didn't go there immediately, though. Liz and I remained behind to close down our Cockeysville apartments, while Mike and Paul went ahead to spring training camp in Arizona. And since none of the Oakland wives called to welcome us, as Byrd Grimsley had after the Montreal trade, my first contact with Oakland was with the players themselves. We'd agreed to fly to California on the team plane between Baltimore and Oakland in late April. During this game I finally faced up to an earlier fear: how would it feel to cheer for a strange new team? I was so used to the bird and the orange-and-black colors and to Earl Weaver and all the rest. Now, with no warning, I must shift my allegiance.

The Oriole front office forced the issue. We wives had always received bright red VIP tickets to sit in a special family section behind the screen at home plate. But today our tickets were green.

"Liz, look!" I cried. "They've changed the ticket colors this year." Halfway down the grandstands, near third base, I realized this wasn't the truth: we were heading toward the visitors' section!

We took our place among Oakland fans and watched our new comrades, the Athletics, go trotting across the field. There was scant but enthusiastic applause all around. Who should I clap for? I wondered. Was I for Baltimore or Oakland? I couldn't decide.

Then Mike, Paul, and Don came out in crisp green and gold uniforms. Fans throughout the stadium began to roar and rise. Soon everyone in the park was standing up!

Mike smiled, tipped his hat appreciatively, and raised both hands. I realized suddenly they were cheering just for him! Fifty thousand saluting fans, stamping, applauding, waving goodbye. My husband had done the job for them, and they were sad to see him go. For a brief moment, I, too, felt sad.

But the plane ride after the game was a rare treat. Professional ballclubs like to claim they can't afford the expense of wives traveling with their husbands on the road. The truth, we all knew, was that no one wanted us. It would severely limit a married player's ability to fool around, since any wife observing such behavior might prove more loyal to the player's wife. All clubs routinely excluded wives from their chartered flights, and most did not allow wives even to buy our own tickets when the team flew commercial. All, however, permitted girlfriends to fly charters, sometimes at half-price, and at a player's whim.

On the plane I couldn't see anything. I had heard about relief pitcher Rollie Fingers's wide handlebar mustache that curved far out to the sides. I craned my neck but couldn't find him. I also looked for Sal Bando: was he really as short as he looked on TV? But all I could see were players I didn't know, reading, playing cards, dozing off, or flirting with stewardesses.

Across the aisle sat Liz and Paul. Paul was leaning back against a cushy white pillow, his eyes half closed, while Liz waved her hands and talked on and on. After each game Paul replayed every inning in his head, speculating on alternative outcomes if he'd done this or another player had done that. He was unlike other players who could turn off a game when it ended. He was the "boy who came to play," caring little for contracts, status, the adulation of fans. All Paul Mitchell wanted was to play baseball. Fortunately, Liz was his perfect partner. She worried constantly about money matters and handled all their business and investments. A more competent, trustworthy manager he could never have found.

Later in the flight, I got up for a walk. Liz had left her seat, and I thought I'd find her and invite her to join me for a visit to the cockpit. I recognized more players as I moved down the aisle: pitcher Vida Blue, infielders Bert Campaneris and Gene Tenace. It was like moving through an animated wax museum: so many celebrities I'd seen on TV, all doing simple, human things, not like stars or heroes at all. Once and for all, I sealed the lid on my illusions about superstars. They were just men like my husband, trying to do a job as best they could.

Near the front of the plane, I found Liz. She was somehow wedged into a corner seat beside the A's manager Chuck Tanner.

"We're a very friendly club," he was telling her. "You'll like it here, little lady. You really will." He'd had a couple of cocktails, so he didn't realize he was being a little overbearing. Liz had been trying to thank him and get back to her seat, but he kept jabbering about how friendly Oakland was. He also blocked her escape with his long legs. Liz looked up at me like a helpless child.

"You're really going to see the cockpit?" she said. "I'm going with you!" Somehow she jumped up then and pulled away. Tanner sat there grinning contentedly.

"Yessir, I know you'll like it here," he boasted again. "We're the friendliest club in the league."

Why Liz Mitchell and I became good friends is hard to say. For one thing, she was a chronic worrier, and I was not. With me, the future was more like a dream: I felt certain Mike was approaching Big Success and that my goals of a loving family and fulfilling career would soon be met. Liz, instead, fretted constantly: would Paul make the team? Would he have a winning season? Would they buy that house she wanted? Be financially secure? But unlike me, Liz had seen her husband bouncing around the minors as recently as last year. She recalled easily how the bottom could suddenly rise up and slap you in the face.

In 1973, Paul had been the Orioles' number one draft choice, the minor league pitcher Baltimore's management thought most likely to succeed. The minors are ballclubs for training future major leaguers. They are almost always owned by teams in the majors. Liz, who had struggled there, thus had a different perspective from my own. I had been fortunate—I had been able to learn and enjoy the big leagues from the start. Mike's minor league days had, when we'd met, been fully behind him. Liz and Paul, instead, endured real hardship—subsistence wages, low prestige, and godforsaken boring towns like Rochester and San Jose. Players generally earned $500 a month, and even the club's manager might make little more. They endured broken buses and a scarcity of bats and balls, while their wives nourished ulcers in the stands and kept a sharp eye on every play and pitch. The wives also watched that stone-faced big-league scout a few seats away very closely. At all costs your husband must strain and overplay in an effort to impress that grim judge, because nothing you did down here mattered, nothing at all, except a trip to the "bigs."

"I took out all our money," one wife told me, "on the day my husband was called up. I just withdrew it all from the bank and flew off to be with him. His tryout could've been his only real shot. So, if he ever needed me, it was then."

Paul Mitchell had actually been one of the lucky ones. His bonus had been $30,000 simply for signing that initial contract, while many players received sums of only $3,000 or $4,000. Though the O's had placed him immediately in the minors, he had received constant encouragement from their coaches to work his way up. Paul, like Mike, had become an "investment."

Even so, it took him three years to get to Baltimore. With moving expenses, lodging, and transportation costs, even that healthy bonus dried up sooner than he and Liz had figured.

The dearth of dollars was by far the hardest test. Some wives took full-time jobs to make ends meet. Most, though, did not, since it would prevent them from attending many games. Instead, expenses were cut by sharing housing, child-care, automobiles, and clothes. But such arrangements went only so far, since the minors were notoriously insecure. Once, Paul had been sharing a rental car with a teammate who was suddenly given his release. Paul exchanged the car for a cheaper model, but on his way home, a tire blew out, the driver's door jammed and the heater began blasting cold air! Paul turned the heap around and managed to get it back to the lot. He decided not to replace it. What was the point? He couldn't possibly afford a good one. Later, pitcher Don Stanhouse lent him a slick Ford Torino, an extra car Stanhouse now owned as a result of a cleverly negotiated new contract with the Dodgers. This kind of minor-league camaraderie often saved the day.

One wife who deserved a medal of honor for the most inventive solution to the money problem was Sharon Hargrove. Although her husband Mike was to become the American League's 1974 Rookie of the Year, his bonus on signing had been only $1,000 just two years before. With a salary of about $100 a week, he and Sharon had been continually strapped for hard cash.

"No matter what you pay your cleaners, it's too much," she told his manager at the Geneva Rangers. "Give all your uniforms to me and I'll wash them every day for half the price!" Mike then stayed late after every game to collect shirts, pants, towels, and socks, which Sharon then bundled up and stuffed into jumbo washers at the corner laundromat. Even better, she often found loose change in the players' pockets, so much in fact that sometimes it would finance the entire load, transforming her fee from the club into profit, free and clear.

I always had the nagging suspicion that Liz's minor league struggles had made the difference in her marriage to Paul. If you married your husband when he was mere potential, with no money, backing, or record of achievement, you were banking on the possibility he'd make it, but also painfully aware he might not. Wives like Colette, Jeanine, and me could never be completely sure we hadn't been more dazzled by our husband's flashy image than by the man himself.

In Oakland, Liz and I were the rookies, or more precisely, like the wives of rookies. Knowing no one else, our friendship blossomed.

What brought us ever closer was the new apartment complex where we now lived. Mike and Paul had come out early and found apartments in a Bay Area suburb called Walnut Creek. Like most Bay Area towns, Walnut Creek was clean, safe, and spacious, with bristling palm trees, clay tennis courts, and manicured lawns. Our apartments, too, were whistle-clean and roomy like everything else: twelve-foot ceilings, slim, tall windows with gold frames, beige walls, celery green and beige striped drapes, and plush gold carpeting. At first glance, the guys thought Walnut Creek was a pretty good choice.

But during their first road trip, Liz and I discovered one feature our husbands had overlooked. Stepping out for a dip in the pool, we realized that most everyone sunbathing and playing backgammon was a man! Many were young and virile, too, with skimpy bathing trunks and well-developed builds. Others were in their late fifties and older, but all smiled cordially at us and nodded and stared when we passed.

Many of these men were gay. But others, Liz and I discovered, were hip swinging singles. They never saw our husbands—Mike and Paul rarely joined us at the pool—so they naturally assumed that Liz and I were single, too. The first few weeks, then, we were constantly approached or leered at. Gradually, we made them realize we were indeed married. Liz, in particular, was glad to have it end: she always seemed pursued by frisky suitors who had won medals of honor in World War II!

108

Much of the time, Liz and I stayed in our apartments. We'd talk till early morning and drink champagne or watch TV. I understood then why some wives in Baltimore often kept to themselves, with rock music blaring and the smell of marijuana seeping from under their doors. You needed help getting through these lonely times; you often hated to leave each other, sometimes wishing you could stay together permanently like real sisters. My friendship with Liz took me solidly into a most important adjustment to this life as a player's wife: coping with the solitude. I no longer felt the urge to bolt home to my parents in Montreal whenever Mike went away, as I had thirteen times the year before. I had a true friend to help me now. I had Liz.

As with Liz, I had known Jo Baylor in Baltimore, though not well. But as the new kids in town, the three of us soon became close friends.

Jo was the most self-assured woman I'd ever met. She had long straightened hair and huge round eyeglasses that constantly slid down her nose. She was never afraid to speak up. Since she and Don were black, she would climb all over anyone who took them lightly.

"Excuse me, ladies," an usher once called to us. "There's a black gentleman looking for you over by the clubhouse." He'd meant Don.

"A *black* gentleman?" Jo jumped. "If he was white, would you have called him a *white* gentleman?"

Jo had a three-year-old, Donny, Jr., whom I always considered a "miniature man." Donny often sat with us and enjoyed a glass of white wine and tried his best to review that day's game. He knew all the players and their positions, and he loved to stand up and hold his body exactly as his father did at the plate. If we mentioned a particularly exciting or dramatic moment from the day's game, Donny would cry, "Oh, wow, right! What a play!" He was a delightful example of the kind of joyful spirit that could be passed down through a baseball family. I was glad to see it.

Unlike most baseball wives, Jo was extremely ambitious. She worked very hard at positioning herself so she could return to school and one day become a lawyer. To me, Jo's motto seemed to be: "If I want to do it badly enough, outta my way, sister, I'm comin' through."

Her husband Don was a fast-rising outfielder who one day, we all knew, would make big bucks. But Jo wanted more than to be a big-name ballplayer's wife. She had a sense of pride about her own identity, too, and she wanted to prove herself. This was a second reason why I appreciated knowing the Baylors. Jo was the first baseball wife I'd met who saw the need for achievements all her own.

By midseason, Liz, Jo, and I were inseparable, going shopping, meeting for lunch, wine tasting, and in general just helping each other out. We went job hunting together, too. One afternoon in a cafe, after watching Jo fill out various applications, I watched some San Francisco models stroll in and sit down in the next booth.

"I wish I could get a modeling job," I sulked.

Jo cried, "Well, what are you waiting for? Just get out and do it! You could model while Mike's on the road, or during weekdays when he's home, and still go to night games."

It was simple and sound advice—I had only needed a little push. I collected my portfolio and soon landed a few jobs. Her pushing was only one of the ways we wives would substitute for our husbands. We also helped each other with transportation, or Liz and I would baby-sit Donny, or we would simply be around for conversation or a sympathetic ear.

Sometimes, though, we got in situations we didn't expect. Like the day a very hip-looking young man appeared at Jo's door. "Hello, Mrs. Baylor, how ya doin today?" he said. He had gold chains around his neck and a very splashy open shirt showing his hairy chest. "Want some flank steaks today Mrs. Baylor? I got a real special on chicken kiev!"

Jo began ordering from him and told us when he'd left he was her wholesale meat man.

"A meat salesman door-to-door?" Liz cried.

"Well, you know," laughed Jo, "we're in California!"

The next month she ordered a box of ribs and found a small carefully sealed brown package inside. The salesman had told her he'd left her a little something extra, but she naturally assumed he'd meant extra meat. Unwrapping it, her mouth dropped. He'd left cocaine!

"How'd you like my free sample, Mrs. Baylor?" he asked on his next visit. "There's more if you want. Primo stuff."

But Jo said, no, she'd just order meat. Thanks, anyway.

"Oh, that's cool, that's cool," he said, winking at us all. "You're the customer, you know. Whatever you say!"

About this time, I realized that, for ballplayers, having fun was something that usually happened off the field. Although baseball was supposed to be a game, not until the final out did the guys revert to kidding, playing jokes, or fraternizing like teens. The game itself held just too much importance.

At a party at the home of Gene Tenace, I watched Mike and his teammates drinking together, joking, playing backgammon. A baseball season altogether is 200 days, so, to get through it, our husbands needed very durable senses of humor. "Off the field, they've got to enjoy themselves," one veteran's wife said. "With the tremendous pressure they have, this may be more true for baseball than for any other sport."

I later heard of some of the ways the players managed it. On road trips, for example, they ran wild, hiding each other's clothes, dueling down hotel corridors with shaving cream, heaving wastebaskets of water or soda out windows ten or twelve stories high. Many times, they'd move all the furniture from a teammate's room, hiding it in a laundry room or out by the pool. Just as often, the perpetrators would remain hidden themselves, and the player would never find out where his stuff had gone.

Even crazier was the night a player came home and found his roommate quietly reading a magazine in a big, cushy easy chair. The player had been drinking a little that night, so he kept focusing and refocusing his eyes. Was he really seeing what it seemed? His roommate, and his chair, were lying sideways on the floor! In fact, the entire room was sideways and the player himself seemed to be standing on the wall. The roommate, however, only casually looked over and mumbled hello.

"I almost fainted right then and there," the player said later. "Only I didn't know which way to fall!" Not for another three hours did his teammates come by and admit they had placed everything—bed, dresser, TV—on its side while the player had been out!

Another time, a player returned one night to his room aching for a nice hot bath. Entering the bathroom, however, he found his tub already filled—with shimmering, lime Jell-O! "Who did this?" he demanded, running up and down the corridor, banging on all the doors. The next day, three teammates confessed. But they kept paper bags over their heads and disguised their voices to protect their identities. The victim, they knew, could easily retaliate on the next trip.

The strongest example of a player's need to socialize with his teammates came from the Reds' great catcher and utility player, Johnny Bench. Bench got married in the mid-seventies, but apparently couldn't bear the thought of going on a road trip of any kind without one of his male friends. The result was that he invited an infielder along on his honey-

112

moon. It was reported in the press that they spent a great deal of time playing Ping Pong in the hotel's game room. Worst of all, especially for his bride, Bench and his buddy played many of those Ping-Pong games the very first night of the trip—Bench's wedding night!

As the newest celebrities in the Bay Area, Mike, Paul, and Don received special attention from the media. Besides interviews and invitations to public events, they sometimes guested on TV shows. One show in particular was a half-hour cooking program in which a respected local chef named Loleck presented male celebrities each week who prepared their favorite dishes on the air. Mike chose tournedos with shallots sautéed in butter. Paul decided on stir-fried vegetables with hollandaise sauce.

From the beginning, Liz and I were a little concerned. Our job was simple: sit at a special table and let our men cook and serve. Loleck would provide running commentary and then help us eat and evaluate. He didn't realize, however, that Paul, though an outstanding pitcher, was not terribly adept at preparing food.

He did love to eat, though, no question he could really pack it away. But when it came to cooking, the Mitchell household in general was not very ambitious. Liz absolutely hated to cook. She and Paul spent many evenings after a game eating with Mike and me. I cooked for them so often that Paul occasionally joked, "Nothing special tonight, Danielle, just make sandwiches. I'm not really that hungry!"

So, as Paul stirred the vegetables, I prayed he'd take it all step-by-step. Paul's attention span could sometimes be short. If he started thinking about last night's game, he'd be in big trouble.

Bending over the stove, he peered into a pot of steaming

carrots. Then his tie flopped straight down and wavered over the burner's bright flame.

"Your tie, pull in your tie!" I wanted to yell, but we were on the air! I just bit my lip. The tie began to singe a little, but he still didn't notice. Just before it could catch fire, he moved aside. I wiped my brow.

Soon, everyone sat down and we began to eat. "This is all very good," Loleck commented. "What herbs did you both use?" Mike began to answer, but Paul continued to eat. During meals, he often went into a kind of overdrive. He was a growing boy, after all: he needed fuel.

One of Loleck's waiters arrived with a bottle of fine Bordeaux wine. He leaned toward Paul. "Care to taste the wine, sir?" he said.

Paul looked up from his plate. "Nah, I don't like wine," he said. He covered the top of his glass with his hand. "I'll just have water, thanks." Then he hunched over again and began shoveling in more food.

At home, even with dinner guests, Liz might have bawled him out. But they were now on TV. She gave him a surreptitious kick beneath the table.

"Yowww!!" he jumped, forgetting where he was. "What'd ya do that for?"

"We're on TV, Paul," Liz whispered. "Come on." Her microphone caught every word.

Loleck was at a loss and the stage crew began giggling and raising eyebrows. But we got off the program without further incident. Liz, Mike, and I had been sweating profusely and were glad it was over. Paul, however, was not bothered in the least. Completely unconcerned with image or putting on airs, he'd enjoyed the experience and above all the meal.

"Hey, that was fun," he said, smacking his lips. "We gotta do that again!" Then he noticed our pale faces. "What's wrong with all of you?"

114

*   *   *

Despite these adventures, I was feeling more and more like settling down, starting a family. I worried, though, about raising children with my husband away so much and an uncertainty about how long we might stay in one place. In Oakland, I at least had a few good examples that it could really be done.

The best of these was Sal and Sandy Bando. Unlike many of the players in Baltimore, Oakland's third baseman was a man who didn't mind admitting that baseball was by no means his only love. Sal actually shared the raising of their children with Sandy, gathering them for picnics and movies and driving them to the dentist or to school. And they attributed their strong partnership to a new involvement with Christianity, which had also become important to many of the other families on the team.

Many of the Oakland ballplayers had achieved their personal goals by the year Mike and I arrived. After three straight world championships, they enjoyed high salaries, enormous prestige, and an envied record. Yet, as with many other top players around the league, an undercurrent ran below the surface: had their struggles been worth it? You could only buy so many tailored suits, drive so many Mercedes, take so many trips to Bermuda. After a while, a sense of emptiness set in. Many players and their wives filled that gap by becoming Christians. Even Liz and Paul got into this born-again movement as the year went on, especially after Paul told Sal: "It's easy for you to get involved in these Bible studies because God has answered all your prayers." To which Sal replied: "The truth is, it's harder for a rich man than for a beggar because the rich man can't believe there's anyone above him."

Much of the momentum for the Christian movement in Oakland came from the wife of one of the team's coaches. She

115

and her husband were born-again Christians who warned continually against high flying.

"You have to remember," she once told the players' wives, "that fame and fortune are not enough. You need a foundation in life, a foundation that doesn't move. The foundation I personally believe in is the same yesterday, today, and tomorrow: it's the Word of God." She often passed out spiritual writings, too, words of wisdom, she felt, to help us all stay grounded.

"Above all," she'd say, "support your husbands. Their jobs are very important to them. When a wife fails to make friends with her husband's career, it creates a wall between them. If you resent your husband's career, your children might grow to resent it, too. So stay by his side—it's your job!"

Though Bible studies never attracted me, the splendid sight of close families definitely did. At last, I was seeing families who had managed it, watching superstars and their wives succeed, and I promised myself that for the rest of the year I'd observe their methods closely.

One day, a former stewardess, Bev Stock, the wife of Mike's pitching coach, showed me her gold bracelet. Her husband Wes had given it to her in his rookie year, 1959.

"Gold bracelets were a tradition back then," she said. The player and his wife would commemorate each succeeding year in the majors with a new charm, usually a replica of part of his uniform. Wes had given her little gloves, bats, balls, and even shoes. But one year she could not figure out the latest charm.

"What is it?" Bev asked, holding it closer and closer to her eyes.

"Just part of my equipment," Wes shrugged. "Though a most important part."

Suddenly, she knew. "Don't tell me!" she cried. "A gold jockstrap!"

116

Wes shrugged again. "Like I said," he replied. "Part of my equipment."

About a year or two later, at a banquet, Bev showed the charm to ex-Yankee manager Casey Stengel.

"Edna," Stengel called to his wife. "Come over here and look at this girl's bracelet." As Edna Stengel struggled to identify it, Casey laughed so hard he nearly fell out of his chair.

When I first saw Bev's bracelet, I worried. It seemed so much like a testament to the priority of her husband's life. Bev had joined baseball in an earlier era, when wives were expected, as that coach's wife in Oakland had put it, to consider their husbands' careers above all else. There was too much else to do, what with raising a family and cheering from the stands. Careers for players' wives at that time were completely unheard of. This realization weakened my confidence: were all my notions of a separate career simply impractical?

In Bev Stock's time, there'd been no doubt. As with Susan Palmer, wives in the fifties and sixties dressed to the hilt: white gloves, nylons, pearls, and high heels. And like many of the wives today, they'd stayed home with their kids until summer vacation, then packed everything and everyone into the car in June to join their husbands in the team's home city for the rest of the summer. The result of all this submission seemed to be the kind of closeness I'd seen in the Belangers the year before.

They also took one of today's rules to its extreme: not only did they try to protect their husbands from many domestic problems in order not to upset them, they also tried to refrain from arguing with them during the season—about anything!

When Wes was still a player, Bev ignored this rule one day but soon regretted it. Wes came on to pitch in the eighth with the bases loaded and ended up walking in a run and losing the game.

"I'm so sorry," said Bev after the game. "I argued with you today; I shouldn't have."

Feeling just as bad, Wes could only look away. "You know I can't pitch when I'm upset," he complained.

At the time I knew her, Bev had teenage sons. When they were younger, she'd struck a deal with them: if they behaved during the games, they could visit their father in the clubhouse when the game was over. As a result, they usually behaved pretty well, gradually growing up to be attentive and courteous fans. One son, Jeff, even became a pro athlete himself with the Seattle soccer team. After one of his games, his father visited him in *his* clubhouse.

"Now, Dad," Jeff said with a solemn smirk as his father came inside. "While you're down here, please sit on that bench over there and don't bother the players; if you want something to eat or drink, just ask me and I'll get it for you." Wes could only grin. It was the same speech he had frequently given Jeff and his other boys ten years before!

Mike and I both learned a lot more in Oakland about pitching and the game itself. One thing we learned in particular was how often some players cheat. Since the Athletics were so good, many of the opposing teams pulled out every stop possible to beat them. Using binoculars to steal signs was common, as was hollowing out bats and filling them with cork to make the ball travel farther. More than even this, greatest of all in fact, was the widespread use by pitchers of the spitter.

The spitball was a pitch with which Mike was not wholly unfamiliar. In Baltimore, pitching coach George Bamberger had been a notorious spitballer in his own playing days, and he even invented his own special variety, the Staten Island Sinker. And he was by no means adverse to passing on some of his expertise to the Orioles' pitching staff. One game, in particular, he walked out to the mound during an extremely rough inning and told Ross Grimsley, "If you can cheat, I wouldn't wait one pitch longer." Another time, he told the press, "If you're a pro, you often don't decide whether to cheat based on if it's 'right or wrong.' You base it on whether or not you can get away with it!" His philosophy was that spitballs, though technically illegal, had been, through the years, acceptable weapons.

A spitball is often more than a ball with saliva on it. Some players improved on nature, using Vaseline, K-Y jelly, fly-line cleaner, or some variety of glue or oil. Mike simply called these substances, "grease." The idea was that a pitcher hid one or more of these inside his cap, say, under the visor, or behind his knee, in the seam, or under his crotch, or in any number of other secret spaces. He then adjusted his cap or scratched behind an ear or ran his fingers through his greasy hair or across a seam. This allowed him to surreptitiously apply a small dab of something to his fingers and then to the ball. Then he'd go through his normal windup and pitch as if nothing was amiss. If the pitch worked, the ball would then zing forward like a fastball, all at once jerking sharply down just as it reached the plate. It all happened so fast that very few batters could get anywhere near it. Babe Ruth had been way ahead of all batters back in 1919 with twenty-nine home runs, but when the spitter was outlawed in 1920 as being too hard to control, thus dangerous to those at the plate, Ruth's home run totals shot up to fifty-four in 1920 and fifty-nine in 1922!

As they did with many pitchers, the press claimed Mike used an occasional spitter, but he'd never admit it. Still, he did once shrug innocently and say, "Well, lots of guys use it."

In Oakland, I started realizing how true this was. I remembered Ross Grimsley, for one, the year before had been accused of putting so much foreign matter, or "junk," on his pitches that Boston starter Bill Lee, the only player I'd ever heard of to admit using the spitball himself, said Grimsley should be wheeled to the mound in a garbage truck!

A Dodger pitcher, Don Sutton, later with the Astros and the Brewers, once challenged major league umpires to catch him in the act of throwing illegal baseballs. "If any umpire tries to discipline me," he told one reporter, "I'll take him to court."

A coach with Baltimore, Ray Miller, said, "Sutton has set up such a fine example of defiance that someday I expect to see a pitcher walk out to the mound with a utility belt on— you know, file, chisel, screwdriver, glue. He'll throw a ball to the plate with bolts attached to it!"

The leader of the pack, however, was Gaylord Perry, then with Texas, most recently with Seattle. He was, and is, so masterful at spitballing that he once told Orioles' pitcher Steve Stone he was willing to teach him his entire array of illegal pitching skills. He'd have to charge Stone a fee for this service, however.

"How much?" Stone asked, expecting a cost of one or two hundred dollars.

"It's a very extensive course," Perry smiled. "But I'll sell it to you cheap: only $3,000!"

All this bothered me at first, this rampant acceptance of cheating. But in time, I came to accept it, too. The spitball was an old baseball tradition, and there had never been much incentive, it seemed, to throw it out. There was an official rule against it, sure, and there always would be. But it was one of those things everyone, even the enforcers, chose to overlook.

Fortunately, some people in the league had a sense of humor about it. Before a game against Perry, Billy Martin brought a bloodhound to the park to sniff out Perry's ball bag. Perry himself smelled like a drugstore—standing near him once, I was nearly asphyxiated by his cologne—and his doctored baseballs were just the same.

So Martin brought his bloodhound and set him to work

pawing at the bag, searching for Perry's "extras." He admitted later, however, "It didn't work."

"Why not?" asked a reporter. "Couldn't the dog find anything?"

Martin looked up, frustrated. "Oh, he found things all right!" he cried. "In fact, he found so much he keeled right over there and died. There were so many illegal odors, the damn dog got so excited he had a heart attack!"

So much for crime and punishment.

In June, I picked a strange envelope from our mailbox. It was brightly colored and officially sealed from the Canadian government. Some kind of document, I thought. But I couldn't imagine what.

Opening it, I could not have been more surprised. I'd just received an official invitation to the 1976 Summer Olympics to be held the next month in Montreal. I was to sit in the reviewing stand near the Queen and Prime Minister Trudeau. A guest of the government.

I ran to the house. "Mike, Mike, you'll never believe it! I just got an invitation to the Olympics. And to the grand ball afterward. We'll be official guests."

Mike was blow-drying his hair, but stopped long enough to ask when it was. "The first week in July," I said. He grunted and turned back to the mirror. The first week in July. I hadn't thought of it: smack in the middle of the season!

He suggested I watch it on TV. Didn't I remember I'd been planning to go to Montreal a few weeks later, anyway? We couldn't afford two trips, right? Too bad the invitation hadn't been for August, he said. Even with his income of $83,000, we had to be "careful."

I left him and went into the den. I sat on the couch and stared and stared at the blank TV. Watch it on TV, he'd said.

121

We couldn't afford two trips, didn't I realize that? This was the chance of a lifetime! Why was he acting so cold?

Maybe the pressure from his new status was getting to him, I thought. He was with a championship team now, he was no longer just a young man with potential. He was expected to perform—*expected*. And to win most every time out. Perhaps it was making him a little nuts.

I knew also he hadn't been pleased by my attempts to find work. Most of the other wives didn't do that, go looking for jobs. The other wives stayed home, had babies, cheered for their men. No careers, no official government invitations. Could Mike be feeling pressure to make his wife toe the line?

I also thought of Montreal itself. In some circles, we'd been Monsieur and Madame Gagnon. When we'd lived there year-round, I was the famous one, and he generally walked a step or two behind. Now, three years later it was I who walked behind. Perhaps he feared his status might be diminished.

I confronted him one more time, back in the bathroom. I pulled the whining blower from his ear. "Look," I said, holding up the envelope. "Just look: it's got a government seal. This is a real honor, can't you see that? It's a *personal invitation* to the Summer Olympics!"

He looked, but only long enough to read the name. "Danielle Gagnon," he said. "Don't they know you're married?"

The next month, I watched the opening ceremonies, as he'd suggested, on TV. I could see little flags with *fleur de lys* fluttering everywhere and Mounties on palominos with braided manes, our city had draped itself in *splendeur*. Once I even thought I saw Carmen, and another time I spied two empty seats just a row behind the Queen. Those could have been my seats, I thought.

I considered a term I'd heard, "the fifth base," an anchored destination to which players ran when the game was done. I felt like that today. I was a mere adjunct of the action, I had no right to be on stage myself. Mike could be, and the other players could, but their wives, no matter how special, must stay in the stands. I was in the stands today. I should have been down on the field.

I grew restless after this incident, increasing my modeling assignments and conforming less and less to my expected role. Meanwhile, Oakland kept falling behind Kansas City and even more pressure fell on Mike. Our tensions increased until the whole matter erupted one hot August night.

Mike was returning from a game on the road in which he'd been knocked off the mound early. I thought perhaps I could patch things up by surprising him, as I'd done after last year's seventeenth win. I set the table with a white tablecloth and yellow linen napkins, tall candles and a bouquet of sweetheart roses. I wore a long white lace nightgown with ribbons on the sleeves and shoulders, a big white bow in my hair.

When Mike arrived home, he hardly noticed. He was afraid of airplanes and usually had a few cocktails on board to calm him down. Now he was feeling their effects.

He tried to acknowledge everything, to compliment me on my "nice" dress and table. But reaching for the wine, he knocked it over. The red liquid spread out in an ugly pool through the carpet's pale gold. We began to argue.

By now our arguments were always the same: he wanted me to stay home, have children, forget about my career. For the first time, I wondered if our marriage was worth it. Where was the shy little bear I'd met at Harlow's in 1972?

I recalled a discussion we'd had while driving home one night from one of last year's games.

"Would you say we're having a good marriage?" I'd asked.

"What kind of a question is that?" he said. "You having doubts?"

"Not really," I said. "I've just nothing to compare it with. You've been married before. What do you think?"

He told me of his plan. During the next five years, he'd like to make a total of $500,000. Then, he said, we'd really be happy.

If his salary kept climbing, as it had steadily since his rookie year in Montreal, we'd make that sum easily. But what about the tremendous pressure that came with it? Would another salary increase be better for us or worse?

With contract review coming up, we'd soon see.

In that year, contract reviews, especially at Oakland, created the most tumultuous off-field episode in baseball history. In Oakland, pressure came chiefly from the club's owner, a flamboyant, very successful Chicago insurance executive named Charley Finley.

A vociferous progressive for years, Finley had been an early advocate of the designated hitter, more colorful uniforms, and night World Series and All-Star games. He also built a petting zoo behind left field for children and once convened an Old Timers' Banquet of legendary Hall-of-Famers, including pitching greats like Lefty Grove and Dizzy Dean. After the A's World Series wins, he led slow, proud parades of ballplayers' families through suburban neighborhoods in San Francisco and the East Bay, with shiny black limousines and fluttering little green-and-gold pennants.

But in 1976, Finley was alone in refusing to accept a new concept called "free agency," which essentially allowed baseball players, for the first time, to bargain their talents on the open market. Recent court cases had made free agency inevitable, but Finley had vowed to fight it to the end. In his case, though, "the end" meant breaking up his own team.

In fact, the trade that brought us to Oakland earlier that year was among the first of Finley's plans for that breakup. He had personally called the A's spring training camp from his offices in Chicago, actually interrupting Reggie Jackson's batting practice to give him the news.

"We just traded you to Baltimore," he said curtly. "Good luck." Then he hung up. Jackson was stunned. Like so many of his teammates, he had played championship baseball for Oakland for years. Even so, he'd been forced recently to demand arbitration to receive a salary he believed comparable to players on other teams. When it came to money, Finley haggled and dealt with an extremely heavy hand.

The case of Vida Blue was typical. In 1971, Blue had won twenty-four games, led the league in shutouts, kept his ERA under 2.00, and walked away with the Cy Young Award. Blue was a fabulously gifted pitcher who had thrown a no-hitter the year before, and had a reputation of always being willing and able to come through for you. Many owners and managers envied Finley for having Vida "True" Blue on his pitching staff.

In 1972, then, at negotiation time, Blue asked Finley to pay him what he thought he deserved.

"And how much is that?" Finley asked.

"$100,000," Blue replied.

Finley laughed. "Listen," he said. "I agree you're worth $100,000, but you know what? I'm still not going to give it to you."

Blue was appalled. "But I won twenty games," he said.

"So you won twenty games?" Finley countered. "Why didn't you win thirty?" Winning twenty games, Finley claimed, was not unique.

This was Finley's method for motivating his players: getting them mad at him. The players would then go out and try to show him up, to prove how good they actually were. Blue, for example, achieved twenty-game seasons twice more after this humiliating meeting and became one of the American

125

League's most solid performers. By 1976, Finley's lack of appreciation got to Blue and to most of his teammates. At that point, they decided they'd had enough.

Reggie Jackson, however, had been trying to remain positive. He'd be eligible for free agency at the end of the year, so the least he could do now was give Oakland fans one more spirited year. Before he could even try, Finley had traded him.

This explained why Liz, Jo, and I had never received a welcoming phone call when we'd first arrived. Morale on the A's had plunged very low. Oakland had once been like a cheerful young family, but now all the players and wives were too angry or exhausted to even care. When Liz and I sponsored a party for the wives in July, Sharon Rudi, outfielder Joe Rudi's wife, remarked, "It's so nice to see the wives getting together again. It's been so long."

Players for almost one hundred years had lived under the "reserve clause," a phrase in the standard contract which chained a player—or "reserved" him—to a particular club throughout his career. In the early seventies, players went to court over this clause. Their victory came in 1973, when a federal judge finally declared that a player who served an "option year" by playing without signing or re-signing an actual contract would no longer be bound. He could then bargain with new teams for his services. After this ruling, the owners agreed to a compromise: voluntary elimination of the "reserve clause" in return for limits on who could go free agent and when. Otherwise, they claimed, the wealthiest clubs would soon buy all the talent and create unbeatable dynasties.

At the end of the '76 season, some players, like Reggie and Sal Bando, would officially become free agents and could auction themselves to the highest bidder. Others, like Mike, must wait another year, when they too, after having played at least six major league seasons would be eligible for bigger bucks. And for players' wives and families, free agency meant even more. It was conceivable that secure, long-term lifestyles could now be established. Players would bargain for multiyear contracts as well as money, and this would substantially reduce the anxiety about where you'd be living and working next. Should you enroll the kids in a school in September, only to pull them out suddenly after a trade the next month? How could a wife plan a career? Should a player buy or build a permanent home near his team's city? Dare you cultivate friendships only to lose them after an unexpected trade around Christmas?

Liz tried to ignore this problem and pushed ahead to buy her first home. It had been her biggest dream all along, to settle down and raise a few kids. She took responsibility so seriously that one day, with Paul on a road trip, she located a house, filled out the papers, and hired a moving van all by herself. By the time Paul returned a week later, Liz had to give him directions to his new home over the phone.

Considering that injuries could force retirement at any time and that age thirty usually signaled your declining years, compensation had never been all that terrific in pro sports. Only recently had salaries climbed at all, with Mike's $83,000 near the top of the heap. The players' union had pushed strongly for a minimum wage of $28,000, but this went only a short way in a profession in which the average career span was three to five years. A player's expenses commonly shot out of sight: an extra apartment in the club's home city, moving expenses before and after the season, transportation costs to spring training, and occasional trips home. Players and wives were always buying and reselling their homes.

Liz herself ended up selling this first home the very next year, purchasing a new place in Seattle where Paul was traded

127

(and two years after that, buying their third house in five years after a trade to Milwaukee). She made some money from these deals, but she lost sometimes, too. One year they spent $38,000 on baseball and living expenses, while Paul grossed a mere $2,000 more. He was destined for a very erratic career, constantly up and down to the minors, with winter ball in Puerto Rico to improve his skills. All this cost money. So for players like Paul, free agency would never mean much, but for others, the conditions of family life would at long last substantially improve.

In November, Finley sent us our contract. We couldn't believe our eyes.

"There must be something wrong," Mike said, scanning it again and again. We called Mike's agent Gary Walker.

"As you know, I'll be a free agent after next year," Mike told him, "and yet Charley's sent me a one-year contract and a twenty percent raise." According to new league rules, if Mike played the next year without signing, Finley could cut his salary as much as twenty percent, so this contract awarded him, in effect, a nearly forty percent raise! And since Mike would have served his six years by the end of the '77 season, the contract also liberated him for the free agent draft.

Walker suggested we send him the agreement, and a week later he called us back.

"I don't know," he said, "I've covered every inch of it. I can't find a catch!"

Charley called soon after, and we then understood. He'd forgotten how long Mike had been in the league. He'd screwed up.

"Let's treat this like gentlemen," he pleaded. "Let's tear up the contract."

"Finley," said Mike, recognizing great fortune. "You have to realize: this is not my doing."

128

"Tell you what," said Finley. "Do this little thing for me and I'll send you a year's supply of my chili." Charley claimed to make the best chili anywhere, but since Mike had introduced me to Mexican food, I knew this wasn't true. Now he was offering a year's supply of the stuff if only Mike would return $17,000!

"Come on, Charley, really," Mike said. "You've been promising me your chili since I came west anyway. Back in the spring you said you'd send me a year's supply. I'm still waiting!" Mike laughed. "Besides, mine is better than yours."

Charley could see he was getting nowhere, so he said, "Say where's that little wife of yours? Lemme talk to her."

I got on the phone and he said, "Convince your husband to tear up that contract and not only will I send you my *recipe* for chili, but I'll also get you a nice little warm-up jacket with your husband's name and number on it. Would you like that?"

He was really reaching now, so I just said we'd talk it over with our agent, and we hung up.

By now Gary was convinced. "If he went through all that," he said, "we've really got him. Sign it."

We waited a few days. Charley sent me the jacket, a nifty sparkling windbreaker in Oakland white and gold and kelly green. It had "Torrez" emblazoned on the back and the number 26. The only hitch was that Mike's number all year had been 24. And still no chili.

We signed the contract.

FOUR
NEW YORK

In late April, 1977, Mike was traded for the third time in three years. Charley Finley made an offer to Yankee owner George Steinbrenner, asking for New York pitcher Dock Ellis in an even swap for Mike. Steinbrenner liked the idea and even threw in two utility players. If Oakland had been a step up for us from Baltimore, New York was the top of the ladder. We could climb no higher.

On the day the deal was announced, I was very sick. I had given birth to our son three weeks before and had developed serious complications. By the end of April, I'd been in and out of a coma and a priest had even come to administer Last Rites.

I spent a lot of time in my hospital bed feeling confused and angry. Mike had been wanting a child, particularly a son, for a long time. But when the time came, I'd been alone at the delivery.

I thought back to how happy he'd been when I became pregnant last fall. For a few days, I'd been feeling pretty raw.

Oakland sponsored a "wives' game" that September, but at one of the practices I didn't have the strength to play. I just sat on the bench and watched. At first, I thought the practice itself was making me sick. There was a lot of silliness on the field—pitching golf balls, Whiffle balls, and oranges—and some of the wives got very upset, too, because they didn't get much chance to play. But gradually I realized that the problem was Liz. She'd been sitting next to me chomping on an English muffin. I couldn't take it and within minutes was bolting for the ladies' room.

"Wouldn't it be funny if you were pregnant?" she said, standing over me by the latrine. She kept patting my back while I retched, trying to comfort me and stuffing me with antacid tablets.

I managed to play in the actual game, though. It was wives versus radio disc jockeys, who were expected to swing with the small end of the bat and run the bases backwards. Also, if they swung and missed just once, they were out. Meanwhile, the wives pampered themselves with rules in their favor. Anything outside the infield, for example, was a home run. And there were vanity cases and little stools and cushions at each base.

Each wife played her husband's position. I was not nearly so adept on the mound as Mike, however: one inning, I threw so far from the plate, I hit Chuck Tanner sitting near the dugout, next to all our husbands, who were filming and taking pictures of us.

At the plate, though, I did *better* than Mike. I actually hit the ball, and even made it to first! Then I got crafty and decided I'd steal second. I ran over, picked it up, then started prancing across the grass toward home plate. Skipping over the pitcher's mound, I pushed the pitcher out of the way and broke for home. The umpire, joining the fun, declared me "Safe!" I was so happy I threw my Playtex gloves in the air.

After the game, though, I got sick again. A few days later, a doctor told me why. "Mrs. Torrez," he said, "you're pregnant!" I was overjoyed and knew Mike would be, too.

That afternoon, I took a seat in the stands near the A's bullpen. Mike was pitching that night and our custom—our superstition?—was that I would always sit nearby whenever he warmed up for a game. I sat there very quiet and looked smug. He kept glancing over at me.

"What's that silly grin on your face?" he asked, between pitches.

"Oh, nothing," I lied.

Then, a few pitches later he finished. "OK," he said, "I guess I'm ready."

I smiled knowingly. "Let's go, Daddy," I said.

He didn't react at first, then did an abrupt double take.

"What did you say?" he asked.

"I said: 'Let's go . . . DADDY.'"

His eyes rolled into his head and he staggered back a few steps. Wes Stock, standing nearby, raised his hands to his cheeks, as if to say, "Oh, no!" Then, Mike's catcher threw the ball to him, but Mike didn't even see it. It just whizzed right by, nearly clipping off his nose. He was in a state of shock.

"You mean you're . . .?"

I nodded excitedly. Then he just turned away with a big, dumb smile and slung his warm-up jacket over his right shoulder and lightheartedly ambled away.

A few minutes later, the game began, but he pitched terribly. He threw walk after walk, allowed home runs, stolen bases, even hit one batter on the head. He balked, too, meaning he interrupted his windup. For any pitcher, this is a rare, though serious, infraction.

No matter how badly he screwed up though, he continued to grin. Once he even walked in a run, then looked up at the chorus of boos from the stands with a very weird smile. By the time Chuck Tanner walked out to him, he was dreamily float-ing back and forth across the mound. He didn't care.

"What's wrong with Mike today?" Liz asked.

"Maybe it was what I told him before the game," I said, biting my lip. I explained that I'd told him about my condition.

"You did *what?*" she cried. "Danielle! You *never* tell such a thing before a game! Look what you've done to him! And to us!"

Tanner signaled to the bullpen and Mike skipped off the mound to the dugout. His ecstatic grin spread from ear to ear. He had pitched a whole two thirds of an inning.

Mike went off to spring training, February 21, 1977, and I stayed in Montreal. Every day he called to see how I was. Once he called while I was watching us both on a taped TV interview. The program's host was questioning us about base-ball "behind the scenes." When the camera zoomed in on us from the side, I could see I was finally beginning to show. With Mike hundreds of miles away, this made me very lonely. I went over to the TV, spread my arms, and hugged the screen. Mike's dark gentle face came on in a close-up, and I began to cry. He was always somewhere else.

The phone rang then, and it was Mike. I told him what I'd just done.

"Well, don't do it again!" he laughed. "That set's too big; you'll get stretch marks!"

He related a little baseball news, and we hung up. The TV show ended, too. Now I could neither talk to him nor see him. He was gone once again. Once again.

From April to October, baseball rules all. Liz once told me, "You've got to time your babies for the off-season and get married in the off-season and get divorced in the off-season. Baseball always comes first."

134

That sounded extreme, until I began to observe it for myself. I saw countless examples of players who could not be present for their children's birthday celebrations or even their births and who missed the funerals of close relations. Los Angeles' Rick Rhoden even pitched a game once despite just hearing the news that his brother had died the day before in an auto accident.

"It was the toughest thing I ever did," he said, after pitching a 4–3 win. "But the truth is I never really considered *not* pitching."

Another time, a minor league outfielder with Salem, Virginia, Alfredo Edmead, crashed into an infielder as both chased a fly ball. Edmead had an extremely thin skull, and the collision killed him instantly. He died right there on the field. Play for that game stopped, of course, but the league refused to suspend a game scheduled the next day, the day of the funeral. League officials just didn't consider the event that important.

There was also the time I received a letter from a wife I'd known whose husband had been traded to Milwaukee. Their baby had died only three weeks after its birth. She followed this news with the line, "Well, at least my husband had a good spring training." She wasn't being callous, though. It was simply the way baseball sometimes makes you think.

But not always. The Salem players, for example, did attend Edmead's funeral after all. Though he badly needed the game's receipts, the opposing team's manager humanely agreed to postpone the game till a later date. Texas owner Brad Corbett once flew Mike Hargrove to the funeral of Sharon's father, then flew him back afterward in time for the same day's game. And Cleveland manager Dave Garcia often remarked to his players, "Don't even thing about coming to the park when your family is in trouble. No baseball game is more important than that."

A very touching example of baseball people banding together in time of tragedy involved Kaye Adair and her bout with cancer. Kaye's husband, Jerry, had been a star infielder for thirteen years with Kansas City, Chicago, Baltimore, and Boston. Kaye and Jerry had become close friends with other baseball couples, like Mary Lou and Kansas City manager Whitey Herzog (later with the Cardinals), Norma and San Diego Padres manager Dick Williams, and Bev and Wes Stock. Their friends, though scattered throughout the country, rallied to help.

"You have to love people while they're alive," Kaye had once told them. So they all pulled together to give support.

"We telephoned constantly," Bev said, "and just tried to be available. But there wasn't a lot we could do. We just wanted Kaye and Jerry to know we cared."

Despite such humane incidents, it was hard for me to accept the fact that baseball usually reigned supreme. As with funerals and other tragedies, giving birth also took a backseat to the dictates of the game. Liz, Connie Robinson, and Jeanine were only a few of the wives I knew who had given birth while their husbands were out playing ball. Jeanine had a good friend in her stepfather, Shelley Richey, an attorney in Tucson. Since Dave was away coaching that year in Cleveland, Jeanine attended Lamaze classes with Shelley, who helped as her moods roller-skated up and down.

"Dave should be here with me," she complained. "Why isn't he?"

Immediately, Shelley said, "Jeanine, you knew Dave's profession when you married him. He's just out doing his job. You've got to accept that."

In early April, I was faced with the same problem. My parents were looking in on me now and then in Montreal, while Mike, who had not yet been traded, prepared in Oakland for opening day. My doctor had just directed me to enter

136

a hospital. He felt sure the baby would arrive the very next day.

"I'm going into the hospital tomorrow," I told Mike on the phone.

"The hospital?" he cried. My pregnancy had been a troubled one, so Mike, without thinking, blurted out, "What's wrong with you now?"

"Nothing's wrong," I assured him. "It's just that it's almost time. The doctor says tomorrow's the big day."

I expected him to leap with joy. But there was a strange, awkward pause. I wanted him to come straight home, and he knew it. But there was a tension over the phone lines, as if he wasn't sure what next to say.

"Well, that's good, I guess," he said, a little gruffly. "What do you want me to do about it?"

"What do I want you to do?" I asked. I was stunned. "I want you to come back, of course. To be with me."

He snapped defensively then, as if he'd been waiting for me to say it. "I'm pitching tomorrow," he said. "It's Opening Day." There was no way, he added, he could possibly come back the next day.

I should've expected this, but even so I nearly dropped the phone. I felt very low, unloved. I'd certainly heard of these moments from the other wives, but I thought Mike and I were different. This was my first baby, *our* first baby! Couldn't he get the day off?

"Danielle," he replied, sounding weary, "you've got to understand: it wouldn't be just a 'day off.' Tomorrow's the first day of the season: I've got to work!" He sounded very torn. Was he angry at me, I wondered, or the situation?

"Well," I said, gritting my teeth, "if you've got to work, you've got to work. But if you can't be here with me, you damn well better win."

The next day, I gave birth to our son, Iannick, while he

137

shut out the Chicago White Sox. My parents and my friend Carmen stayed by my side the whole time, though she said later that for three hours I'd been crying for Mike. When it was all over, I pulled little Iannick to my chest and shielded his eyes from the bright overhead lights. And I thought: "It's just you and me, little guy. We did it ourselves. Your daddy wasn't here to share the pain, but I hope he can at least get up here for some of the joy." Then I nestled him in my arms and we both fell asleep.

Mike arrived the next day. He said that during the game the day before, in the fifth inning, he'd been standing on the mound preparing to pitch when suddenly the crowd had let out a terrific roar. He had rarely heard one so loud. His catcher, Jeff Newman, pointed to the scoreboard in center field.

"Congratulations to Mike and Danielle Torrez on the Birth of Their Son." I felt two things when I heard about this: how sweet it was for the club to do that, but also something disturbing about 30,000 people getting this news before Mike did. As father, he should've been the first.

Mike's face lit right up when he saw his son. He picked him up and held him close to his cheek, and father and son looked as though they were meant to be side by side always. But Oakland needed the father back. Two days later, Mike left us and returned to California.

The same day, I developed complications. I started blacking out a lot and bleeding heavily, though I refused to tell Mike. In baseball, unless absolutely necessary, a wife must never upset her husband's game. I would pull out of it on my own. Or so I thought, until I was rushed by ambulance to the hospital.

In the middle of all this, Mike was traded. It happened so suddenly, it didn't even register when he told me over the

138

phone. It was only hours before I was rushed to the hospital. "I don't feel strong enough to talk right now, Mike," I said. So my father took the phone, and Mike gave him his news of his new assignment in New York.

Shortly after, my condition took a turn for the worse. I began going in and out of a coma. A priest was called. When Mike telephoned that day, my doctor decided to fill him in. He flew immediately to Montreal to be with me.

However, he was scheduled to report to the Yankees. He had three days to make the transfer, but on the second day, he decided to stay with me until I recovered. On the third day, George Steinbrenner called my room. Mike had not even contacted his new club yet.

"How are you?" Steinbrenner asked me. "All of us in New York are hoping you recover real soon." But I'd never even met him or any of the Yankees. Then he asked if I'd seen Mike.

I literally did not know where Mike was. I'd been unconscious every time he'd come to my room. Even so, after this, I started receiving flowers and get-well cards from the Yankee front office.

It was soon nearly a week since Mike had been traded. The Yankees' manager Billy Martin told the press: "I need this guy badly, but, shit, we can't even find him. I haven't met him yet, and already he's got me upset." New York headlines blared: "WHERE IS MIKE TORREZ?" But Mike kept avoiding them all—the management, the press, the fans. He was taking a very brave stand: he was choosing his wife over baseball. Couldn't they leave him alone for just a little while? Couldn't they let him stay?

"I really don't know where he is," I told Steinbrenner again. "But I'll tell him you're looking for him as soon as I hear from him."

Ultimately, George gave in. He called and said, "Tell Mike

it's OK, we'll let him stay. Just have him come back after the baby's christening. There'll be no penalties."

Once said, the flowers and phone calls all stopped. And soon after, I began to recover. By then, Mike had left for New York. I promised I'd join him as soon as I felt strong.

In mid-June, I made it to New York. Mike had rented an apartment in a high-rise in Hackensack, New Jersey, and, as usual, the choice of furnishings needed a woman's touch for the right coordination. There were mud-brown carpets, brown velveteen chairs and a couch, and a wooden wall unit with trophies, books, and figurines. You couldn't tell where the furniture left off and the floor began. The dining room table was formica, and on the wall was only one hanging—a poorly done oil painting of Mike.

It was a dank, stark bachelor flat when it could've been a fairly luxurious penthouse. There was a doorman in a chandeliered lobby below, and the view from our window afforded spectacular vistas of areas all around New York. At night, lights sparkled and reminded us where we were—New York, New York. We were very close now to Big Success. In the day, though, I'd look out and watch a solitary bird circling listlessly outside. Then, I'd wonder.

Our year with the Yankees was a turning point for Mike's career. He had striven for excellence in baseball all his life, and being with New York was his highest validation. Mike had done very well in '76: he'd won sixteen games and had an ERA of 2.50. He'd even improved his almost legendary erratic control. Where in 1975, he had led the league in walks, in 1976, he'd cut that total by a third. He gave Wes Stock credit for that: he had advised Mike to throw fastballs early on, thus getting "ahead" of the batter, that is, throwing more strikes than balls. Leave sliders and curves till later, Wes said. Mike had taken his advice, and it'd worked out just fine.

But Oakland had not won the pennant, and in New York, nothing else mattered. The pressure I'd seen building in Oakland was even more intense here. With George Steinbrenner around, Mike couldn't let up for a minute. The pressure was now not just to do well, but to do the best of all. The championship of the world, not personal statistics, was the reason he was here.

Mike's nervousness over this got the best of him, and he began taking it out on me. We argued a lot, and he often seemed agitated beyond reason. Nineteen seventy-seven was not a year I could handle it. I remained ill the whole season. Because of my weakened condition, paying attention was very hard. I seemed always to be operating at about fifty percent capacity. Even watching TV was a trial. Add to all this my concern about our son, and we had the makings for a terribly volatile relationship.

Mike was constantly distressed over my condition. Though sometimes he was very sweet and loving, other times pressure from the Yankees drove him up a wall. He became upset more for himself. He wanted to show me off to the other Yankees, to have me by his side at Yankee affairs. But I couldn't always go.

"You're constantly sick," he said once. "We can never do anything or go anywhere." There was little I could say to that. I was not well enough even to think about some kind of strategy for setting things right. It was true, I *was* always sick. But I couldn't help it.

Our strongest disagreements, though, were over Iannick. Our first argument had been about his name. I'd wanted Iannick, a version of John, because it was a very popular name in Brittany, the homeland of my father's ancestors. Mike, however, had wanted "Mike, Jr." I objected strongly. I was afraid our son would grow up a clone.

141

"What if he wants to be a hairdresser, or a gardener or something?" I said. "I don't want him to have to live up to his famous father's name."

I'd heard stories about such problems before. Bev Stock had related one about her son's pitching for a Little League team. He'd done quite well one year, perhaps too well.

"We think it's not fair for the Stock boy to be pitching in this league," the other parents said. "He's been professionally coached."

They had a meeting and tried to bar him from the league. They felt Wes had been guiding his son with some sort of magical advice. The truth was that Wes had been on the road so much, that times together with his son had actually been few and far between. In fact, he'd only seen his son play twice! Perhaps some of Wes's ability had filtered down to the boy, but the accusation of "professional coaching" was way out of line. To keep peace in the league, though, Bev counseled her son to give up pitching and just concentrate on his bat. If he walloped hit after hit, as he was capable of, the other parents would be hard-pressed to protest: in nine years in the majors, Wes himself had a whopping total of three base hits!

Many of our arguments derived directly from Mike's very masculine self-image. Like many players, Mike had an obsessive fear that his son might not grow up to be a "real man." All the players seemed to feel this way: Dave Duncan, Kenny Singleton, even easy-going Paul Mitchell. The possibility that a player's son might one day become, say, a ballet dancer was terrifying. At the mere suggestion, their eyes would ignite. "No way," they'd say. "Not my son."

Because of this, Mike objected to the way I fed and dressed Iannick. I saw no harm in draping a two-month-old child in white linen nightgowns, but Mike would reproach me, saying, "Just leave him in his pajamas." Also, I was always trying to keep him clean and free of germs, though I admit now maybe

I was being a little too compulsive about it, as my mother had been with me. So Mike would say, "C'mon, let him get dirty once in a while. You'll make a sissy out of him." Sometimes I'd laugh at these comments, since Mike's voice would betray that he wasn't being completely serious.

The limit, however, was when Mike tried to teach him to drink beer. That was the way they did it in Kansas, he said, so why not here?

"We're not in Kansas anymore!" I snapped. "I don't want you to give him any beer ever again!" Meanwhile, Iannick, who had taken a few sips, observed us contentedly from his high chair with slightly glazed eyes.

Our arguments reached a peak over the issue of bringing Iannick to the park. "I want my son at the games," Mike insisted. He wanted to show Iannick to the other players.

As I'd seen back in Baltimore, baseball people were by no means adverse to raising their children in the stands. Changing diapers, singing them to sleep, breast-feeding. It was necessary if the mother was to attend any of the games.

Sometimes, this could be fun. Mike Hargrove had originally played under Billy Martin in Texas, and they'd become good friends. After Sharon had a baby a few years later, she brought the infant down to the seats behind the dugout and called for Billy to come out and see him. Martin accomodated and Sharon held up her son.

"What do you think?" she asked.

Martin just shook his head. "I was afraid of this," he said. "The kid looks just like me."

My own recollections, though, of bringing babies to baseball games was much more grim. Put simply, the very idea scared me to death. I recalled the first time I'd watched an infant in the stands. His mother cradled him protectively as he slept, but suddenly someone belted a high fly ball and everyone jumped up. Many fans then began screaming and hollering, and the baby's eyes snapped open. The loud sounds scared him and he started to cry. I wished instantly that his mother had left him home.

Another time, an overzealous fan accidentally dropped his Coke all over a three-month-old girl. Also, games were often cold at night and hot in the afternoon sun. And in New York especially, there was cursing, drinking, fighting, and clouds of marijuana smoke. At Iannick's young age, I just couldn't buy the idea that the ballpark was the place for him to be.

Though I agreed to take Iannick to an occasional game, for the most part that year, I watched them at home on TV. And despite all the pressure on Mike, what I saw him accomplish was a very good summer. He won fourteen games for New York (plus three more for Oakland before the trade), including a solid ten straight during the heat of the pennant drive in August and September. If he had set out on joining the Yankees to prove himself, he couldn't really complain. He'd really done well.

He was in admirable company, too. The Yankees were a pretty strenuous test. So much dazzle here! Everything about the place was so damn big! The stadium was brassy and new, having been remodeled two years before, and the personalities in the organization were larger than could be believed. The fans, too, were as boisterous as they came. Even the wives' lounge was something magnificent: wall-to-wall carpets, a big TV monitor, a security guard, private bath facilities, and sparkling new furniture. A far cry, indeed, from the days of standing in the autumn frost in the parking lot at *parc Jarry*.

And the names on the Yankee roster put my superstar illusions to the test once again. Here were characters in a public novel that raged on the nation's front pages nearly every day: the battle for authority between Steinbrenner and Billy Martin; the colossal ego of home-run king Reggie Jackson; the

144

shenanigans and practical jokes of reliever Sparky Lyle; the sparkling defensive moves of third baseman Graig Nettles; the quiet, stolid leadership of Yankee captain, catcher Thurman Munson. Feuds, historic feats, wild times. These Yankees were unlike any other team I'd ever seen or heard of.

Manager Billy Martin, in particular, was among the most colorful. He'd been a tough street kid in Berkeley, California, who had gone on to play with the Yankees of the 1950s. This meant friendships with Joe DiMaggio, Casey Stengel, Mickey Mantle, and Whitey Ford. And during these years, Martin developed a reputation, especially while hanging out with Mantle, for doing everything—both work and play—with frenetic zeal.

Once, for example, Martin and Mantle both got into a major fracas because of a brawl in a Manhattan nightclub. The members of an Ohio bowling team were vacationing in New York and began hurling racial epithets in the nightclub toward the performer, Sammy Davis, Jr. Martin became infuriated and stormed over and began poking the beefiest of the bowlers in the chest. Next, a punch was thrown at Martin, and Mantle came rushing to his aid. Before long, the two Yankees and the Ohio bowlers were mixing it up real good.

Another time, Mantle and Martin had been out carousing in Boston. "Holy Jesus, Mick!" Martin yelled, looking at his watch. "It's almost half-past eleven! We gotta get back to the hotel."

By the time they got there, however, the Kenmore Hotel was closed up tighter than a drum. In those days, doors were locked promptly at the Kenmore at 11:30 p.m. Martin and Mantle then began skulking through a side alley, rummaging for another way inside. Finally, they piled up garbage cans and trash and clambered up toward the second floor. Then they wriggled carefully through a tiny open window. It was neither their first, nor last, missed curfew.

145

Mantle himself, one of the game's all-time greats, was a maniac all on his own. Arriving at the ballpark one day dead drunk, manager Casey Stengel directed him to sit on the bench and skip that afternoon's game. In the ninth inning, however, only Mantle's skills as a home-run hitter had any chance of winning it for New York.

Casey shoved a bat in Mickey's hands and pushed him out to pinch-hit. "Swing at somethin'," Stengel barked.

Mantle teetered to the plate, then glared toward the mound. Two pitchers, he believed, were out there, both of them winding up to throw. Then, all too suddenly, two fast-balls came bulldozing their way toward the plate. Closing his eyes, he swung with all his might at the closest. He connected, and the ball sailed miraculously out of the park.

Staggering as best he could toward first, he slowed down as he reached the base. "Turn left! Turn left!" the Yankee bench began to yell. Somehow Mantle managed to navigate all the way around, finally tottering over the plate and making it official. The Yanks had won!

Even notables as great as Mickey Mantle, however, were eclipsed in 1977 by the personalities of the current stars. This was most dramatically illustrated by the Yankees' newest slugger and perennial egomaniac, Reggie Jackson.

In 1976, with Baltimore, Jackson had spent the entire season checking out other teams. He knew he'd be a free agent at the end of the year, so he was trying to decide where he next wanted to go. Kenny Singleton said that Reggie had told him in Cleveland, "There's no way I'll ever sign here. Not enough reporters around."

After coming to New York, Reggie made the mistake of telling a reporter that, from now on, he would be, by far, the most important individual on the team. "I'm the straw that stirs the drink," he said, implying that the team captain Thurman Munson should no longer consider himself the Yankees' leader.

Munson, a quiet, firm man, resented this at once. A feud resulted, and for the rest of the year, though the Yankees functioned well enough to maintain first place, feuds like this one, and also the one between Martin and Steinbrenner, would dominate much of the action. News stories reported spite, enraged arguments, and personal breakdowns. Pitcher Dock Ellis summed up everyone's attitude by remarking, "Every time we make trouble, ol' George flies out here from another part of the country and gets in our way. Maybe we should make a *lot* of trouble, so he'll keep flying out here. Sooner or later, his plane's gonna crash."

Fortunately, there was a lighter side to all this. Probably no player in modern baseball was more famous for jokes and kidding around than the Yankee's main relief pitcher Sparky Lyle. If a birthday cake was delivered to the locker room, Lyle would immediately undress and sit on top of it! He also wore fake casts on his pitching arm to scare his coaches, and he once nailed a teammate's shoes to the floor just before it was time for the player to leave. He also filled a deodorant canister with glue one day and left it out where he knew Yogi Berra, the Yankees' lovable coach, would pick it up and use it. Poor Yogi couldn't get his arms unstuck for a week!

"Some people say you have to be nuts to be a relief pitcher," Lyle explained. "But the truth is I was nuts before I ever became one!" For the players' morale, Sparky Lyle's humor was greatly in demand.

As with other teams, the wives were something else again. Many were as demure and shy as those I'd seen in Oakland, Baltimore, and Montreal. But there was an overwhelming new factor here as well. It was something I hadn't encoun-

147

tered in such magnitude ever before: cattiness. Here in New York, competition was as brazen as it could be. Everyone wanted to get ahead. This was so important to some of the wives that looking good, even if it meant making others look bad, was a high priority.

Once, in the wives' lounge, we were playing charades while waiting for the guys. This particular night, first baseman Chris Chambliss's wife, Audrey, started poking me in the ribs with glee. I had submitted the name of the opera *Carmen*, and one of the wives on the other charade team had just selected it.

"They'll never get that one," she squealed. "We're gonna win!"

As expected, the wife was stumped. She stood there foolishly for a few moments, struggling to imagine how to begin.

"Hurry, hurry," urged her teammates. "Time's running out."

"I know, I know," she snapped nervously. She was at her wit's end. "Just shut up and let me think." She tapped her foot desperately trying to come up with something.

Finally, with only ten seconds left, she began gesticulating wildly, indiscernibly. There was no way to tell what she was trying to convey.

Time ran out and my teammates exploded with delight. Hers, though, went crazy.

"Who or what was that?" they cried. It was the first time in the game someone hadn't gotten one.

The woman, however, was furious and shot back, "OK, whose bright idea was this?"

I raised a meek index finger as Audrey jumped up and down. "We won! We won!" she cried. "And 'Frenchie' did it!"

The wife looked at me with well-honed derision and said, "You idiot—no one could have gotten that one. No one! You don't even play fair. How could someone like *you* think of an opera, anyway?"

Everyone got very still. Suddenly, there was tension in the room thicker than brick. I didn't know what to do.

"You fool," the woman went on. "You don't even know how to play this game. What are you doing in this country, anyway?"

The wives dispersed. Audrey, like a good friend, maneuvered me to another part of the room. I hadn't meant to embarrass anyone. I'd thought I was just playing a silly game. But the woman had been all geared to fight back. From this I learned that, in New York, I must be always on guard.

I'd seen this kind of thing before in Oakland, though nowhere nearly as fierce. There, many of us who were starting pitchers' wives resented reliever Rollie Fingers. Whenever he came into a game, it seemed he promptly gave up one or two runs. If these extra runs tied the score, it made the entire game a fresh slate. This meant, then, that the new pitcher, the reliever, would receive credit for the victory if the team ultimately won. We grew suspicious about Fingers since, after those first couple of runs, he always settled down to shut out the opposition the rest of the way. The result was that if Oakland won, Fingers would then acquire the official victory for himself.

Our husbands told us we were crazy to think like this. "No reliever would act that way," Paul Mitchell maintained. But we couldn't help thinking it. Unlike the players, the wives sometimes had a very difficult time with team spirit. Wins were money and we naturally wanted our husbands to get all they could. So somehow, though both Fingers and his fiancée, Danielle, were the nicest couple you could hope to meet, we kept believing that they were conspiring to steal from us.

149

With such hidden resentments, there was always the desire to put people down or embarrass them. It was a portent of things to come. In this regard, Oakland had been a little mound of discontent, while New York was a tumultuous volcano. There was money to be made in the Bronx, big money, and there was also vast prestige, glamour, and limitless fame. The Yankee uniforms did not have commanding dark blue pinstripes for nothing. If your husband dropped a fly ball or allowed too many hits or struck out at a crucial moment, you might suddenly have a hard time making simple conversation. Your "friends" in the wives' lounge became too preoccupied even to look at you. In Oakland and Baltimore, there had been chiefly hidden resentment. In New York, as I'd seen playing charades, it sometimes spilled right out.

There were a few wives I liked, though. Utility infielder George Zeber's wife, Dusty, was one. She was extremely honest and considerate, and we sat together at the games and visited each other's homes. I also liked Audrey Chambliss. She was a gorgeous black woman who had once been a model and who still kept up with the latest styles.

I was also fond of shortstop Bucky Dent's wife, Stormy. A pretty southern girl about as pure as you could ask, she and Bucky were like two freshly scrubbed farm kids from the cover of a box of corn flakes. Originally from Georgia, they'd spent the last four years with the White Sox in Chicago. They'd moved around, though, even more than that. Whenever I fretted about our three moves in three years, I had only to think of them: trying to make Bucky's career happen, they'd moved forty times in seven years.

This year was their first with the Yankees. I guessed that maybe that's why they'd seemed so pure. No time yet for sophistication and cool. Whatever the reason, I sincerely liked them both.

*   *   *

One blessing in 1977 was that Mike didn't get hurt. The pressure was on to play and play, sometimes in complete disregard for the player's health. This could mean playing with slight sprains or bruises or something worse. And there was always the underlying fear of some major injury happening without warning. Billy Martin, for example, in his playing days, once broke his leg simply sliding into second base.

Players also develop serious conditions that can never really be corrected. Reggie Jackson came down with back problems that would flare up constantly throughout his career. Sometimes his health would be magnificent; other times, he'd be playing with very sharp, shooting pain. Once a reporter, observing Reggie's play during one such attack, commented, "When Reggie's back is hurting, he looks, in the outfield, like an arthritic trying to pick up a dime off a bathroom floor."

Risk of injury was even worse for a pitcher. Arms could swell up, shoulders could tear apart. Once in Oakland, I saw Mike's arm balloon to twice its size after pitching thirteen innings. After the game he spent two hours soaking it in the locker room and another hour at home from 1 to 2 A.M. Days went by before the swelling disappeared completely.

Pitchers treat their arms with very gentle and precise care. Wearing warm-up jackets on the field as they do, to prevent colds in the muscles, is only part of it. They rarely lift heavy furniture or boxes at home and they often soak their arms even when they're healthy, to keep them loose. Mike also made sure to throw at least a few minutes every day between pitching starts and to exercise regularly during the off-season. A pitcher's arm is his fortune, his whole life. If he or anyone else mistreats it, his career is through.

One thing that disgusted us in 1976, the year before, was the Tigers' treatment of their Rookie-of-the-Year pitcher, Mark "The Bird" Fidrych. Although Detroit finished far out of contention, Fidrych himself was an extravagant success.

Nine hundred thousand fans came to see him that year, both for his nineteen wins and his eccentric activities on the mound. Fidrych used to talk to himself (and to the ball) between pitches, construct little sand castles on the mound, and run across the field to congratulate his fielders when they made a fine play. The fans loved him and his antics.

Tiger Stadium was filled to capacity each time Fidrych pitched, so there was great pressure on him never to miss his turn, despite knee and shoulder problems. The result was that Detroit drained him to the bone. They used him like a pitching machine. Mike felt very bad about it. Two years later, we would see how sad it all really was. Fidrych's health problems got so rough he had to sit out a full season and then return to the minors the next year. He hasn't been back since.

In Oakland, Wes Stock told us that ninety percent of pitchers develop sore arms and other inflammations as a direct result of the strain of their jobs. Bill Campbell, for example, a fearsome Boston relief pitcher, once tore his "rotator cuff," a muscle in the shoulder which permits the arm to move and "rotate." Campbell's arm just completely died one day as he attempted to throw. It just hung at his side, limp, and there was no way to make it respond. Tom Seaver, who had once watched Campbell firing his ninety-mile-an-hour fastballs, remarked, "Throwing so hard like that you'd eventually turn your arm into a noodle, anyway."

Seaver, meanwhile, was Campbell's exact opposite. He liked to work steady, not fierce: what he lost by not throwing hard, he gained in control. Thus Seaver rarely developed serious difficulties. In fact, the only major injury of his career involved not his arm, but his back, which he threw out once while picking up a half a case of wine in his basement!

Another common pitching injury involved bones grinding against other bones, wearing out cartilage. A Cincinnati pitcher, Paul Moskau, played a full year with these kinds of problems developing. To the concerns of his wife, Anne, he'd keep saying, "What can I do? The team needs me." But eventually he had to stop playing and give his arm months of rest.

How much had the Reds' organization really cared about his dedication? The Moskaus found out when the season ended. Everyone on the Reds was preparing for an exhibition game to be played in Japan. Everyone, that is, but Paul and Anna.

"He can't play so he can't go," the Reds' management declared.

"But Bill Bonham's going," Anna protested. Bonham was a new pitcher with the team who was well liked and had contributed a lot to the team's success. But near the end of the season he'd also hurt his arm. It was even in a cast.

The Reds' management replied coldly: "Well, sorry, but we already included him. We're not changing any plans. Paul can't go." It must be added that the Reds management is notorious throughout both leagues for being tremendously inflexible. Still, these stories about Fidrych and Moskau said something to me about playing your heart out and risking your health. Wasn't there a responsibility from your employer to not abuse you?

I remembered the terror on Patty Foli's face when Tim had broken his jaw that day back in Montreal. Or the helplessness that Janie Roberts felt when her husband, Dave, now an infielder with the Phillies, got hit in the eye by a bad hop and almost lost his sight. The ball just smashed up at him, too sharp and quick to grab or block, and knocked him instantly to the ground. He lay there for a moment not moving, and Janie, watching on TV, could do nothing to help.

But Dave at least got up that day and resumed play. The same was not true of Houston infielder Art Howe. One day he faced Montreal pitcher Scott Sanderson. A fastball screamed in at him at over ninety-five miles an hour and struck the side of his batting helmet, bashing in an ear-protector and rico-cheting down and off his jaw.

Watching at home on TV, Art's wife, Betty, heard the crash of the ball's impact very distinctly over the announcer's mi-crophone. Then she watched as Art's legs buckled and his body melted to the ground. "Oh, my God," she gasped aloud, "I've lost him!"

The Expos' catcher, Gary Carter, caught Art as he fell, then trainers from both teams rushed out, followed by some men with a stretcher. Art lay still, not moving an inch. "He seems to be completely unconscious," the announcer said.

Betty peered as close to the set as she could. If he'd only move just a little, just once, she thought. They then began carrying him off the field.

Thankfully, just before he'd been taken off camera, Art shifted one of his legs. Thank God, Betty sighed, he's still alive.

Minutes later, the club's traveling secretary called her. "He's conscious now," he said. "In fact, he's not as bad as we thought. The doctors say, after a week or two, he should be fine. His jaw will be wired, but he'll be up and around, and he may even be able to play." Relieved, she hung up. But the TV then ran replay after replay of the accident, and in slow mo-tion. Then more replays that night on the news and here and there on news broadcasts throughout the next several days. For a long time after, whenever a ball came too close to a batter's head—any batter's head—Betty felt immediately very ill.

The same thing affected then Red Sox manager Don Zim-mer. It was said that one thing Zimmer would never do was order any of his pitchers to throw a beanball. The reason for this was that Zimmer, in his playing days, had been hit by the Twins' Jim Kaat, later a star with the Cardinals. Zimmer had been knocked unconscious, then fell into a coma that lasted

154

several weeks. Today, though fully recovered, he walks around with a metal plate in his head where the ball struck.

I'd always worried about Mike being injured in the same way: a hard smash back to the mound, and Mike falling to the ground, badly hurt. In fact, something like this actually had happened in Baltimore. A line drive had thundered back and hit him on the arm. The impact of the ball was so hard its stitches etched themselves deeply into bruised, purple skin. It was weeks before both the markings and the pain on Mike's face as he tried to sleep disappeared.

Then, years later, pitching against Baltimore, he was hit again by a ball hit by his old friend Kenny Singleton. It crashed right at him and this time hit him in the head. An inning later he began to feel dizzy and was rushed to the hospital. It must have killed Kenny to be the one to hit such a ball. Fortunately, X-rays revealed that Mike was fine.

Some players have a habit, and a reputation, for getting injured all the time. Cindi Roberts's husband, Leon, an outfielder at that time with Houston, gave one hundred percent effort and was frequently named to the *Sporting News* "All-Hustle" team. Much to Cindi's dismay, Leon was famous for being able to challenge anything, even outfield walls—and win! Once, he broke his wrist chasing a fly ball into such a wall. For the next week, he couldn't even lift their nine-pound baby, Cindi recalled, let alone swing a bat. Even so, a mere ten days after the injury, he was back in the lineup. And playing just as hard.

If it is difficult at times to assess how appreciative baseball's management is over this kind of dedication, it can at least be said with certainty that pitchers, like Mike, appreciate it a lot. And as a pitcher's wife, I did, too. It can mean significantly more victories for a pitcher and, thus, higher pay. So if a player was willing to try that hard for my husband, I couldn't help feeling good about him. It was the flip side of the Rollie Fingers situation: if a player made my husband look good, I'd naturally take a strong liking to him and his wife. But there were those players in the field who seemed not to try at all. Oakland outfielder Billy North had this reputation. He seemed always to be moving too slowly and missing fly balls. Although players would rarely say a word to him, many of the Oakland wives boiled over with rage at his sloppy play. I remember one day in particular when a game had been lost because he'd moved at half-speed and botched an important catch. After the game, he came back to the clubhouse and passed a group of us standing in the hall. He always had an excuse when he played badly, like a sore arm or a sprained ankle. We were pretty upset that day, but, of course, we wouldn't say anything, either. It just wasn't our place. But he knew what we were thinking.

He passed us in the hall, dragging his left foot. He had his head down, but he suddenly looked up into our eyes and our disgusted faces.

"It was my TOE!!" he shouted.

Then he limped away.

By September, Mike's ten-game win streak helped the Yankees pull in front of Boston and Baltimore for full control of first place. New York had won the pennant the year before, and now, with Mike's help, it looked as though they'd take it again.

The race went down to the next-to-last day. Boston was playing Baltimore at Fenway Park, while New York was meeting Detroit. No matter what happened to New York, if the Sox lost that day, we'd clinch the pennant.

It was a tense afternoon. After about three innings, the New York game was delayed because of rain, and it was decided that the game would be resumed only if Boston won. Many of the wives then began leaving their seats. This was not typical behavior, and even stranger, they were not coming back. Later, when Thurman Munson's wife, Diana, got up, too, I got very suspicious. Diana was a very pretty, long-haired midwesterner, unfailingly peppy and loyal. Thurman was the players' captain, and Diana, I guess, was unofficially captain of the wives. Absolutely no one disliked her. She had a way of getting us all fired up about play on the field. Despite our many hidden animosities, we sometimes resembled high school cheerleaders, all because of Diana's enthusiasm.

So, after Diana left the stands, I decided to see for myself where everyone was going. In the lounge, I found a cluster of wives around the TV. They were watching the Red Sox.

"The Sox are behind!" Audrey Chambliss said, not taking her eyes off the screen. The Sox had been ahead, she said, 5–1 in the fifth, but had since blown their lead. They were now trailing in the bottom of the ninth, 10–9!

Stormy Dent was there, too, quietly watching, and also outfielder Lou Piniella's wife, Anita, and Sparky Lyle's wife, Mary Lou. Diana was there, of course, but out of character: she was leaning back languidly in one of the lounge's dark purple chairs, barely watching. "Ohhh," she murmured softly, "I hope they lose."

I stepped away from the TV for a moment to get a Coke. Suddenly, the wives burst out in horror! Audrey grabbed me by the arm and pulled me back.

"Look, look," she cried. "You gotta see this!"

Someone with Boston had just cracked a hit, and a runner was in scoring position on second base. It was the tying run. In some ways, we were still miles and miles from clinching the pennant.

All the wives leaned forward. "No, no," Diana Munson said quietly, watching closely now. The Sox outfielder Jim

Rice was up with two outs. Rice had hit twenty-five home runs the year before, so he was not someone we took lightly.

"C'mon, c'mon," Audrey said, teeth clenched. "Make him whiff."

The Oriole pitcher leaned back and threw. Rice eyed the ball, shifted his hips, and swung away. The ball shot to the sky.

"No, no," Diana said again, rising from her seat. "Catch it, please catch it."

We all stopped breathing. The ball went straight up over the third baseman's head and came plummeting back down. Then it dropped neatly into the infielder's upraised glove. Jim Rice had popped out. The Sox had lost.

"We made it! We made it!" the wives cried. Diana jumped straight up like the cork off a bottle of champagne. "We're number one!" she yelled. "We're going to the Series!" Soon all the wives were cavorting wildly, hugging each other, kissing, then skipping back to the stands.

"I can't believe it!" Dusty Zeber exclaimed.

"L.A., here we come!" shouted Stormy Dent.

Many of us had our arms around each other as we danced up the aisles. For the first time all year, we were actually a happy, unified group. We were on our way to the top! I was as proud of my husband as I thought I could ever be!

Before the World Series are the playoffs. Each season, four divisional championships are won, two from each league. In 1977, they went to New York in the American League East and Kansas City in the American League West; and to Philadelphia in the National League East and to Los Angeles in the National League West.

The Yankees beat Kansas City, but it was no easy task. The Royals knocked Mike off the mound in the sixth inning of Game Three and won, 6–2. Then Mike pitched in the middle innings of Game Five. With Sparky Lyle's help, the Royals went down, 5–3. The playoffs ended with New York winning three games to two.

As I sat in the stands watching these games, I began making comparisons to the Mike Torrez I'd met five years before. He was much fatter, like a baked potato on two thin sticks. His hair was much longer, too, spreading out from under his cap. But this change in physical appearance took nothing away from his ability. When Mike pitched these days, he pitched very well. In fact, he made the whole process look unbelievably easy. His fastball was clocked at eighty-eight miles per hour. If he was struggling to attain this speed, he didn't show it. He always looked so calm, relaxed, steady. He seemed to be finally on his way to achieving the excellence he'd always desired.

This would be helpful, of course, when the season was over. Mike had been negotiating for most of the year with George Steinbrenner for a new contract. If dealing with Charley Finley had been tough, jousting with Steinbrenner was the Impossible Dream. Steinbrenner treated his employees like glorified slaves. His front-office turnovers set new records.

Strangely, I never thought of Steinbrenner in quite the same way as his image portrayed him. In person, he always seemed friendly, affable, even a little humble. He could laugh at himself, it seemed, he didn't always play the wild-eyed, fiery businessman everybody claimed he was.

Once, at a team party held at his private club, I watched him circulate to every table and joke and chat with the players and wives. He talked about more than baseball, too, unlike many players who usually recounted stories from a game and not much else. I remember him talking with Mike and me about his favorite restaurants in New York, about traveling around the country, and about his family. I also recall looking at how he dressed—very conservatively, with an executive-style mohair wool jacket, starched white shirt, and pressed slacks. He also had very shiny, polished black shoes, a feature I knew most men overlooked. He seemed quite concerned with making a good impression.

Even so, Steinbrenner wanted things done exactly as he asked. He once fired a secretary for bringing him his tuna sandwich a few minutes late. He demanded vast amounts of loyalty, though he was often quite short on this quality himself. If he gave a player his word that he'd keep him on, it was not uncommon that the player would be gone, usually traded, the next week. Managers and coaches came and went.

Billy Martin, in particular, got into shouting matches with Steinbrenner more than once that year. Steinbrenner loved to telephone the dugout and say things like, "Tell Munson to shave his beard or I'll fine him $500." Or, "Take Nettles out of the lineup. He's just not doing his job." Steinbrenner would then cite statistics to back up his ideas. "Piniella's only batting .167 against Cleveland left-handers," he might say. "Bench him till the Indians leave town."

Martin, however, wouldn't take it. He was the type of manager who believed it was his job, and no one else's, to run the team. So he kept hanging up on George or screaming at him to leave him alone. Once, he cursed into the phone, then pretended he didn't believe it was really his boss. "Imagine that," he told a few players after he hung up. "Some guy just called impersonating George!" Finally, he got fed up with George's calls and grabbed the phone and literally tore it off the wall.

This, of course, set George off, too. The year 1977 was filled with newspaper accounts of blowups and near-blows. Finally, to get George off his mind, Martin began to drink and came close to a nervous breakdown. The year after we left New York, 1978, Martin, on the verge of quitting anyway, was fired.

160

During the 1977 season, Mike asked George for a six-year contract of $2 million. Since he was eligible for the free-agent draft at the end of the year, he was not being unreasonable. In the first draft, the year before, the Yankees had paid $1.99 million for six years with Cincinnati pitcher Don Gullett. Also, Mary Garland, whom I'd known in Baltimore, watched her husband Wayne sign a ten-year contract with Cleveland for $2.3 million. The money was out there.

The Yankees laughed loudly, though, when Gary Walker proposed Mike's demand. "He'll never come close to two million," cried Gabe Paul. Then: "Listen, we'll give him $400,000 tops. Believe us, Mr. Walker, that's a pretty darn fair deal." Gary disagreed. By August, he and Mike broke off the negotiations. They'd take their chances in the draft.

The World Series opened at Yankee Stadium on the evening of October 11. The Dodgers had beaten Philadelphia three games to one and had led the National League in both home runs and ERA. They were formidable opponents.

In five years of baseball, I'd never seen such commotion. Police and security guards stood on all street corners and gates. There were wooden roadblocks around the stadium, and fans with helmets, noisemakers, bullhorns. Usually, I'd see jerseys and hats with emblems from nearly every club in the majors. But this day, all clothing and paraphernalia proclaimed only one set of options: you liked the Yankees or the Dodgers, no one else.

I drove carefully through the crowd in our big blue Cadillac and I felt hot and cold, calm and tense. The movement all around was dizzying. I tried singing along with the radio so people outside wouldn't know how scared I was. So many arms, legs, curious faces. I couldn't stop looking at them. And they kept looking in at me, too, so I began to worry that they

161

might be able to get inside the car somehow. It was like rolling through a cattle field in an empty 7-Up can.

Inside, Yankee Stadium looked and felt like an old-time American political rally. Red-white-and-blue banners hung everywhere. Politicians, actors, athletes from other sports, well-known models and fashion designers, famous musicians occupied box seats and more expensive sections in the grand-stands. I saw men in three-piece suits wearing baseball caps and women beside them in $800 outfits waving pennants. The crowd also glimmered with flashes from diamond rings and jewels, as lights cascaded from the high overhead towers and from the camera lights of the TV crews. There was also a wide cross-section of races: Chinese, Indians, Hispanics, many blacks. It was a grand festival, a breathless extravaganza. And the stage was out there on the grass, between two long, straight chalky lines.

I'd thought of the first two games of the World Series as no more than an extension of the playoffs. Mike wouldn't be pitching till Game Three, so I assumed they wouldn't be overly interesting to me. But with the crowd clamoring for victory, with the fever rising, I realized that this assumption was way off. How the Yankees did during the Series would affect our status, income, personal satisfaction. Though it was often hard during the regular season to take as great an inter-est in games in which Mike didn't pitch, this time it was different. These first two games would matter a lot.

In Game One, then, I cheered heartily for Don Gullett and Sparky Lyle. Happily, they combined to beat Dodgers Don Sutton and Rick Rhoden, 4–3 in twelve innings. In Game Two, however, I cringed the entire game. Dodger Burt Hooton struck out eight Yankees and won with ease, 6–1. The Yankees were favored to win overall, but the Dodgers had always been known for scrappy, don't-count-us-out baseball. They would by no means be an easy mark.

162

With the Series tied, then, Game Three became vital. It was imperative that the Yankees win and take the Series lead. In baseball, gaining even a slight lead is considered an important psychological edge. Thus, Mike, the scheduled starter, faced perhaps the biggest challenge of his career.

We flew on a specially chartered plane to Los Angeles where Game Three would be played. I joined the other wives in an unofficial fashion show up and down the aisle. Making the World Series automatically meant extra paychecks, and many of us had wasted no time in spending as much as we could. Each player received a bonus for winning the league championship, then another for the Series itself. So, when our husbands gave us some of this new money for ourselves, we'd bolted immediately for Tiffany's, Bergdorf-Goodman's, and Saks Fifth Avenue.

On the plane, I wore a glittering diamond necklace and a blouse with a ruffled white linen neckline. Mary Lou Lyle modeled an exquisite diamond ring with marquise-shaped canary yellow diamonds. Other wives wore flowered skirts, lavish watches, and shining black cossack boots. If we were married to champions, why not show it?

This plane ride was far more subdued than the one on which I'd flown from Baltimore to Oakland. Players' wives were aboard this time, and this made all the difference. Much less flirting with stewardesses and fewer off-color jokes. It was a happier flight, too, because we'd made the World Series. Everyone felt terrific!

Publicity about the Series reached its height by Game Three. We read both the New York and Los Angeles papers every day. For the first time since I'd been a player's wife, I realized how we wives were little more than the decoration on a cake very important to the rest of the world. Photos showed us in the stands with glossy lipstick, white pom-poms, continual smiles. One picture showed Dodger wives Cyndy

Garvey, Patty Sutton, and Gunnar Hooton with big rah-rah white carnations, long flowing tresses, and deep eyeshadow. All three waved giant blue pennants.

I was particularly intrigued by Cyndy Garvey. Like Susan Palmer back in Baltimore, Cyndy had always projected herself as the perfect little wife of an even more perfect star. In the photo, she was dressed impeccably as always, this time in a white turtleneck sweater and brown leather jacket. With her sugary blond hair, she had the look of a woman whose marriage could never feel the slightest strain from this game. But some of us knew otherwise.

Word had slowly dribbled out, through the press and through the wives' grapevine, that their life was not, in fact, the pure joy they'd presented. One interview in particular had Cyndy saying, "Steve has to take advantage of his peak earning years, but God, sometimes I just wish I had someone to cuddle with. Baseball wives are told how lucky we are, and we're not ungrateful. But I have to have someone to talk to at night. Steve is gone ninety-two days a year. In the off-season, he's busy with business affairs. Sometimes you just crave conversation."

She also related a story of how she and Steve had once brought their daughter to an emergency ward with a broken wrist. Scanning one of those interminable hospital forms they had had to fill out, the admitting nurse said, "Oh, your husband's a baseball player? What team?"

Steve was standing off to the side and didn't hear. The Dodgers, Cyndy replied.

"Really?" said the nurse. She was now even more curious. "What position does he play?"

Their little girl needed medical treatment right away, and this nurse was talking baseball! Cyndy got very upset. She grabbed the form and flung it at her husband. "You deal with

164

her!" she exploded. "She's obviously more interested in you than our daughter!"

Around this time, the *New York Times* also published a full article on the Yankee wives. It ran with a photo very similar to the one in L.A. This time the public saw Kathy Gullett, pitcher Ron Guidry's wife Bonnie, and Diana Munson. As usual, they displayed gleaming teeth, fluttering pom-poms, and a cheerleading air.

In the article itself, "Mary" Torrez was described as wearing a white silk, gilt-edged dress. At least they'd got the dress right! Also, Audrey Chambliss, the article said, wore a midnight-blue velvet pants suit. She was quoted, too: "We have no way to release our pent-up emotions," she said. "The men on the field can run and curse. We have to sit here and grin."

If Audrey was letting the cat out of the bag a bit, it was not outside her style. Audrey, like Jo Baylor, was tough and outspoken. The problem was that wives were not really encouraged to express dissatisfaction to the press. It was similar to talking back to the fans: bad for the image. Those photos were exactly as the players wanted us to appear to the outside world: happy, supportive, without strong opinions.

Many of the black wives on the Yankees became increasingly irritated with press coverage in L.A. I realized why during Game Three. I watched a white photographer crouch behind a black player's wife and young son in the stands. The photographer leaned over the boy's shoulder, ignoring him, and shot pictures of all the white players' sons. The boy's mother finally said, "You know, my son's a ballplayer's son, too." The photographer shrugged.

"Well, OK," he said, "I guess I've got some extra film in the camera." But the next day, I couldn't find the boy's picture anywhere, nor could I find any pictures of black players' wives in the newspapers the whole time in L.A.

Later, Audrey became incensed about the way all the reporters seemed to congregate exclusively around the whites. She finally told one reporter, "I've yet to see any quotes from black wives since we arrived in California."

The reporter replied: "But I'm not trying to do either a black or white article."

"Well, maybe not," Audrey snapped, "but it still seems that nobody cares at all what we black wives have to say."

Racial prejudice seemed even more obvious when a special "wives' party" was held one afternoon at the Dodgers' Stadium Club. I looked around and realized that Audrey Chambliss and the other black wives were nowhere to be found. I discovered later, from asking Audrey, that she hadn't been invited!

Game Three was Mike's all the way. Frank Sinatra threw out the first ball, and then shook hands with Mike and said, "If you're ever in Vegas, give me a call. We'll have dinner." Mike shyly shook Sinatra's hand and said he would. Except for this brief moment, he was in complete control the whole day. He pitched brilliantly, striking out nine, and clicking with fastballs, curves, and sliders. He even bunted in the fourth inning to advance a run.

Times at the plate, though, were, for the most part, a throwback to days in Montreal. This World Series was being played under National League rules, so Mike was forced to bat for himself. He swung as before, lunging out at some of the worst pitches imaginable, and striking out nearly every time. Once, I turned back toward George Steinbrenner, sitting two rows behind. I gave him my best, most apologetic look. He just covered his face with his hands. "I can't watch this," I could see him say.

The game ended with Mike beating the Dodgers' twenty-game winner Tommy John, 5–3. Mike walked off the mound and raised an index finger, smiling wide. He was number one now, a World Series winner, and the other Yankees embraced him, shook his hand, clapped him on the back. I thought: my husband—today, he's the very best!

In the fourth game, Ron Guidry, a Cajun from Louisiana, fired a four-hitter, and Reggie Jackson hit a home run. The Yankees won again, 4–2, and the Dodgers were now behind, three games to one.

In the fifth game, the Dodgers came back. Don Gullett, who had been sensational in Game One in New York, got shelled this time for seven runs. Thurman Munson and Reggie Jackson hit back-to-back homers in the eighth, but it wasn't enough. The Dodgers won, 10–4. If Los Angeles won the next game, too, it would all come down to Game Seven. So, Game Six was a must. And Mike was pitching.

On the morning of Game Six, back in New York, I felt a strange confidence. This game was as important as any had ever been. Mike didn't seem particularly worried, though. Somehow, it was like the pressure had been building on both of us all year and had now passed us by. It was as if we didn't dare consider what this day could really mean, just like the superstitious practice when a pitcher is in the middle of a no-hitter. No one in the dugout dares say a word, no one wants to chance breaking the luck. If Mike won today, he'd be the biggest of heroes. But if he lost, and if the Yanks also lost tomorrow, he'd be the biggest of goats. It was quite an important day.

The crowd at the game was even scarier than before. The players' parking lot was completely overrun with fans. If the first game had seemed pandemonic, this one was out of sight. New York had at one time been a formidable dynasty, but that was fifteen years ago. These fans wanted those days returned. A win today was a must. It just had to happen.

I got out of the car in the parking lot, as a police cordon held back the crowd. There was only a skinny path from the lot to the stadium door, with hundreds of exuberant fans on either side. I hurried by without looking and hustled inside.

The game began and Mike was in trouble right away. Cyndy Garvey's husband tripled home two runs in the first inning and L.A. immediately surged ahead. I began to hold my breath with every pitch.

New York tied it in the second, thanks to Audrey's husband Chris. He had a homer off Gunnar Hooton's husband, Burt. Two to two.

Before long, Mike's trouble became obvious. He was getting nervous, losing confidence. When things didn't go well, this was his way. He'd start thinking, "I don't have it today, but I'd better find it soon. I've got to show everyone my best stuff!"

I could also see that he'd started to face the catcher! I had told him back in Montreal not to do this, and his pitching coach had said the same. Twist a little to the right, just before the windup, we'd advised. But when Mike got nervous, he forgot. If only I'd had a direct phone line to the mound.

A reporter from the *New York Times* came over and asked, "Any comment on the game so far? Do you think Mike can do it?"

Strangely, I still felt very confident. For some reason, I had a strong sense the Yankees would win. The Dodgers were ahead now, 3–2, having gotten a run in the third inning, but for how long? Some Yankee was going to bang a home run. I just knew it.

"We'll win," I said. Then, kind of nonchalantly, I looked down at a French newspaper I'd been reading between innings and resumed my reading.

168

"You sound so sure," the reporter interrupted. "Can I quote you?"

"Of course, you can quote me," I said. "The Yankees will definitely win this game."

In the fourth inning, Thurman Munson singled, and Reggie Jackson made me a prophet. On the first pitch, he slammed the ball clear out of the park. The Yankees took the lead 4–3. Then, Chris Chambliss hit a routine pop-up that dropped between two Dodgers for a double. Moments later, he scored on Lou Piniella's sacrifice fly ball.

The reporter came back. "It looks like you're going to be right," he said. "It's 5–3."

"Make no mistake," I said cockily. "The Yankees will win the World Series. You can bet on it."

In the fifth, Reggie sealed L.A.'s doom. Again with one man on base, he hit another ball on the first pitch, and again it was out of the park. For Reggie, it was home run number two. The score was now 7–3. The rumble in the stadium was like a long-awaited quake.

I could have guessed it would have been Reggie. I'd always liked him, though I knew everyone else was put off by his gigantic ego and style. For one thing, he loved to drive to the ballpark in one of his $90,000 Rolls-Royces—he had three! Or he'd casually mention at a party he was wearing a $150 shirt or a $400 pair of shoes.

But if Reggie's ego was without bounds, his abilities were as well. He belonged to that murderous tradition of Ruth, Gehrig, DiMaggio, and Mantle. Many fans disagreed, saying that he was not, in fact, "that good." But Reggie would reply: "The only difference between me and those other great Yankees is my skin color." And for that, many Yankee fans would never forgive him.

But today he was doing his darnedest to make them forget.

169

A sparkling new 1978 Lincoln would be awarded to the game's MVP. I had hoped Mike would win it. Now, though, it looked certain for Reggie. Then, in the eighth inning, for the third consecutive time that day, he once again hit the first pitch out of the park. There goes the Lincoln for sure, I thought. The Yankees were now way ahead, 8–3. It was Reggie's fifth home run in three days, and it set an all-time World Series record. The only other player in the history of baseball who had ever hit three home runs in a World Series game before had been Babe Ruth (who did it twice). As Reggie rounded the bases, I looked over at the reporter and winked. Reggie and the Yankees and my husband were about to make it!

In the ninth inning, the stadium was ready to burst. LA had scored one more run. Dodger outfielder Lee Lacy stepped to the plate with two outs. I looked at my tall, husky husband with great pride. He'd scattered nine hits, struck out six, and walked only two. How generous did Steinbrenner's $400,000 look now?

I began to think again about how far Mike and I had come. That goofily dressed young man at the disco in Montreal and his naive teenage blind date. How little I knew of baseball back them, and how little I cared. The years since: our marriage, the trades to Baltimore, Oakland, and New York, and now this exhilarating World Series. Just the right pitch now, just a well-placed fling of that silly white ball and my husband would be at the top of the heap. I held my breath as he pulled his arm all the way back. C'mon, *mon petit lapin*. Make it sing.

I saw mounted police bracing around the field. Fans began climbing across railings and slithering down poles. The whooping in all the sections grew to a steady roar. It was like a major earthquake. Some kind of scuffling broke out in the bleachers, but I couldn't see. Too many bodies yelling and waving arms and pennants blocking my view. Then, my husband, the great Yankee pitcher, wound up.

He threw toward the plate, and the umpire stretched out to his right. Ball one. The tension was maddening. A teenager straddled the side of his box seat, one leg in the stands, the other hovering over the field. Everyone was getting impatient.

I had a sudden fear that someone might bolt onto the field and run and jump on top of Mike. Then a rolled-up program landed a few seats away from me, and some crumpled beer cups cascaded to the field. Thunder from the screaming was deafening. I recalled something Cindi Roberts had said about Leon playing winter ball in Puerto Rico.

"The fans were so wild there," she said, "that one time they didn't like the way the game was going and began throwing things on the field at the players. And I don't mean Frisbees or paper cups. I mean rocks, bottles, bricks!! A policeman accompanied Leon to the outfield. Leon even wore his batting helmet out there. I was pretty scared."

Back in New York, I was pretty scared, too! Mike had best get Lacy out quickly. But again, he looked so calm. He simply leaned back, then pulled his arm forward and threw. Ball two. What was he doing down there?

"C'mon, Torrez," someone yelled. "Get it over or it's back to the farm!"

Suddenly, I remembered. "Turn, turn!" I yelled at the top of my lungs. I knew he'd never hear me, but I had to do something. Maybe I could communicate on some other level. I thought as hard as I could: c'mon, hon, c'mon now, turn away from the catcher. TURN AWAY!!

Mike wound up again and threw still another ball. He still couldn't hear me. How bad could things get?

Suddenly he looked up, squinted toward the stands, and kind of smiled. And just as suddenly, I lost all my fears. He'd heard me! Somehow, some way, he knew what to do. He looked back at the batter, then slowly and confidently turned his body to the right. Then, he cocked that mighty right arm of his and lunged forward. Lacy swung with all he had. The ball popped up high overhead.

Everyone in the stadium sat down. Fifty-four thousand manic Yankee fans, with fifty-four thousand sets of anxious eyes. We all gazed up into the New York October sky. Lacy's ball went up, up, and for a minute looked never to come back down. Certainly it was the highest pop fly I'd ever seen. But edging carefully underneath was my Mike Torrez.

The fans waited for it to fall. Mike waited. I waited. The entire stadium was afraid to breathe. Then, the ball reached its arc and began to descend. People began running out onto the field, surrounding the mound. Mike raised his left hand and steadied an eye. I detected a burgeoning smile on his face, a glimmer of victory. The ball came down, steadily but slowly, dropping closer to victory. Fans began whooping and tossing caps in the air, jumping up and down, hugging madly. Then, all at once, before anyone realized it, the ball plopped with finality into Mike's glove. A half-second later, Mike leaped into the air himself, wearing his widest grin ever, his glove still high over his head, and the ball firmly imprisoned inside. Thurman Munson came running out and threw his strong catcher's arms around Mike's waist, and the two soon were pressed together by the multiplying, delirious crowd. The Yankees had won it! Reggie Jackson, George Steinbrenner, Billy Martin, Sparky Lyle, Lou Piniella, Bucky Dent, Graig Nettles, Chris Chambliss, Don Gullett, Ron Guidry, Thurman Munson. Modern-day champs in the tradition of Whitey Ford, Mickey Mantle, Babe Ruth, Lou Gehrig, Yogi Berra, Casey Stengel, Roger Maris, Joe DiMaggio. And now a farm boy had joined them, my sweet husband Mike Torrez. My

172

husband: the winning pitcher in the final game of the 1977 World Series! My husband.

Thousands poured out of the stands and onto the field like a torrential flood. I saw Mike and all his teammates going crazy with joy, hugging, leaping in the air, dancing wackily. The wives all around me went crazy, too. Everyone was whooping and leaping and pounding on seats. Many of the fans began tearing across the field, ripping out bases, snatching caps from the heads of players, stealing baseballs and bats. It was an all-out riot!

Amid it all, I couldn't move. I was frozen with joy. I had no idea what to think or say. My husband was a two-game World Series winner with the greatest team in baseball. I kept repeating it over and over, my husband and the World Series. My husband, my husband, my husband.

Suddenly, a very authoritative man grabbed my arm. "C'mon, Mrs. Torrez," he said. "We've got to get you out of here." He lifted me from my seat and pushed a wedge through the ecstatic, dizzy crowd. He was a New York policeman and he and other officers were escorting the wives to safety.

I glanced down at the field and saw Reggie barreling toward the dugout like some raging fullback, blocking and shoving everyone in his way. I saw fans tearing at uniforms, grabbing for players' arms, trying to leap up on the Yankees' backs. Then, cops on horseback began galloping across the field and swinging heavy black nightsticks at teenagers and exuberant fans. Clubs came down with full force, whacking and threshing at heads and legs. The fans were amok everywhere: up flagpoles, backstops, and scoreboards. The police moved in with determination to turn them away.

I could barely see Mike. He, too, was being hustled away by a beefy police officer. In fact, that officer looked even bigger than Mike himself. They both disappeared inside the dugout.

The wives were hustled down to a corridor outside the locker room. The whole place was jammed, not with fans but with police, reporters, personnel from the Yankees' front office, and politicians.

"Stay out here until your husbands come for you," the policemen commanded us. A woman reporter squeezed by then and I thought: she can go in, but the wives can't?

I looked at the TV lights flooding the doorway to the locker room. The entire entryway glowed. Then reporters came out and clapped me on the back.

"Tell Mike nice job," they said. "Congratulations." As they passed, I got only more frustrated. When could I see my victorious husband?

Finally, Mike came out, rollicking, bubbling, buoyant. He was drenched in champagne and sweat and he threw his arms around me, messing my dress. But I didn't mind. Not today.

"Thanks, hon," he said. He was so happy he was thanking me, I knew, for just being his wife. Then, he pulled me as close as he could, and we kissed. It was our longest, sweetest, most fervent kiss in years.

Other players came out and embraced their wives and each other and even strangers. They were like uncontrollable little boys on their birthdays: never before had they felt so sensational! I watched Mike strutting up and down the hall, champagne squishing out from his shoes. He had finally made it.

It took a long time before we left that night. Finally, with great reluctance, he said, "I'm going inside now and take off my uniform." I knew he didn't want to. Taking off the uniform represented the players' first step toward letting go of victory. Actually leaving the park came next, followed by getting together with their wives. In fact, by the time everyone had reached the huge buffet and celebration at the top of the Sheraton Hackensack, much of the exhilaration in the air had dissolved. The players were still pretty happy, of course, still recollecting the game, the Series, specific plays. But they also had begun the slow transition back to "normal life." They danced with their wives, ate heartily, and now even laughed and argued and conversed about things other than the game. The Series, very grudgingly, was becoming history.

Still, as I watched Mike go back inside the locker room, I knew his place in this history would never be forgotten. I listened to noises echoing through the stadium walls, whoops and victory chants both scary and sweet. Exultant, careless glee. The Yankees had won the World Series. The Yankees and my husband, Mike Torrez.

FIVE

LAS VEGAS

The World Series changed everything. Mike had been striving for Big Success all his life. Now it was here. We were mobbed for autographs in restaurants and on the street. We were ushered to the front of lines at airports or exclusive nightclubs. We were mentioned in society pages or in gossip reports on TV. Newspapers carried Mike's name, not buried in the middle of an article, but prominently and with his photo. People began asking for my autograph, too: as Mrs. Torrez, I became a far greater star than as teenage model Danielle Gagnon. Both of us had finally arrived.

In November, Mike was named Kansan of the Year. We sat in a convertible, the focus of a long parade, and waved at thousands along Topeka's main thoroughfares. Kansans stood proudly on the sidewalks and cheered and threw confetti and rice. Mike received the key to the city, and we were both guests at a lavish VIP ball with scrumptious Mexican buffets prepared in Mike's honor and dancing well into the next morning. It was a high honor for this one-time midwestern farm boy.

I was glad to be there by his side for these festivities. I had disappointed him in October when New York mayor Abe Beame had honored the Yankees with a mammoth ticker tape parade. On that day, I'd been too sick to go.

"Would I get to sit with you?" I'd asked Mike early that morning. We were cuddling under a warm blanket on the sofa in the living room.

"No, hon," he said. "They've got a bus for the wives."

The thought of riding in a grimy bus with a bunch of snippy Yankee wives was not terribly appealing.

"Will the bus at least be close to you?"

"Not really," he replied. "I think it's bringing up the rear of the parade."

I looked out at the cold, rainy, steel-gray skyline. The thought of all these arrangements made me more ill than I already was.

"Oh, Mike," I said. "I know how much I've disappointed you this year, missing so many games and all . . ."

He raised an index finger to my lips and cut me off. "Just tell me how you feel today," he said. "Do you think you're strong enough or not?"

I said I really wasn't. "Then don't worry about it," he said. The conversation was over. He'd go alone.

I watched the parade on TV. He looked so tall and handsome. He stood up on a colorful platform truck and waved and smiled gratefully at the crowd. I watched, still sorry I couldn't be there. How could he have been so understanding? Even after big Series victories, he still had no wife by his side.

He came home and we watched the parade on a Betamax. It was such a joy, the culmination of all these years of struggle. Mike and three other players in beige raincoats stood in the pouring rain, looking like little boys who'd just entered a gigantic candy store. From time to time, they leaned over and touched the outstretched hands of the crowd lining both sides of the streets. They waved, laughed, and just took it all in.

Standing next to Mike was Lou Piniella. Mike and Lou had become great friends that year, so it was wonderful to see them together now. I remembered how they loved to kid each other about their ethnic backgrounds.

"Aww, you're nothing but a poor, dumb Mexican, Torrez," Lou would say.

Mike would reply, "And they call you 'Sweet Lou from Peru?' Hell, you're one hundred percent Puerto Rican and you know it!" In fact, Lou Piniella was a native of Tampa, Florida!

Thurman Munson stood beside them, chewing tobacco, looking, in contrast, almost blasé. He kept his hands in his pockets most of the time and only occasionally pulled one out for a wave. Right behind him, however, was his nemesis and the man himself, Reggie Jackson. Reggie's home runs had set a World Series record, so he waved loftily to the crowd as if the applause were only for him.

I remembered joking with him at the celebration party after the final game. "Oh, Reggie," I'd said sweetly, "I need a car so bad and you've got so many of them. What are you going to do with that big Lincoln you won tonight?"

Reggie was so self-absorbed, he just looked at me and said, almost sadly, "I'm sorry, Danielle, my sister needs a car, too. I'm going to give it to her." He was flying so high he'd completely missed my joke!

So, as I watched them all on TV soaking in the praise, I knew: it was OK to be self-absorbed after winning the World Series. It had most certainly been earned!

About a month later, Mike and I joined a few of the other Yankees for a junket to Las Vegas. There was a big heavyweight fight that month and George Steinbrenner and some of the players—though none of the wives—wanted to see it badly. I wanted to see Las Vegas.

The area itself really surprised me. I'd expected a glittering cosmopolis sprawling out over half of Nevada. Instead, Vegas seemed a tacky little desert town with cheap hotels, fast-food stops, and only one particularly glamorous avenue called the Strip. On the Strip were, of course, the fabulous hotels and casinos, those grand establishments I'd always heard about— the Desert Inn, the Sahara, the MGM Grand, Circus-Circus. There were also lush fountains and dazzling marquees. But still, the feeling of the place was disappointing compared to my preconceived ideas from postcards and brochures.

This included our own hotel, Caesar's Palace. The front facade of Caesar's was marvelous: a sweeping half-moon driveway with Roman statues bordering a brilliant green lawn and tall white columns at the entrance. Inside, its huge jeweled chandelier glowed like the sun. But our suite was a different story: the walls were covered with a crushed velvet of orange and gold, the carpet was a sickly pink shag, and in the middle of the bathroom sat an obnoxious round Roman tub.

I walked around in a daze, not knowing whether to laugh or cry. Suddenly, Mike grabbed me and pulled me beside him on the bed. Then he pointed to the ceiling.

I looked up. We were both staring down at ourselves from a gigantic ceiling mirror! It spread out to each of the walls and recorded every furnishing and movement in the room.

Mike loved to gamble, so this Vegas trip, for him, was as good as Disneyland. With Lou Piniella, he spent long hours at the crap tables, losing ten dollar chips, then twenties, then a few fifties, then rushing over to the cashier's window and picking up more. At one point, the two got a little frustrated and gave up. They began kicking across the room like little lost boys, until they came upon George Steinbrenner.

"What's the matter with you two?" he cried. The two recounted their bad luck.

"Hey, nothing's too good for my boys," he said. He reached inside his jacket pocket and pulled out a big wad of bills. "Go have some fun," he said, peeling off five hundred dollars. He reached up then and tried to hug them both simultaneously. But he was a little too short, so the movement made his jacket curl up at the shoulders and envelop his neck and head. I was standing off to the side, and the scene looked like two giants being embraced by a stubby, headless gnome.

Mike and Lou spent much of the Vegas trip side by side. Lou was an example of a "new" type of ballplayer. Where Pete Rose exemplified the scrambling, hyper-loyalty of the old-timers, Lou was much more selective with his energy. Frequently used as one of the Yankees' designated hitters, he could often be found during games inside the clubhouse, playing cards, reading, or watching the game on TV. Lou worked hard on the field, his batting average was routinely around .300, but when named the DH, his job became a matter of four or five trips to the plate, and nothing more. The dugout was a cramped space, and since he no longer left for the field every inning, he began feeling stagnant there, and bored. Rather than forcing himself to endure it throughout the game, he preferred the comfort and tranquility of the clubhouse. While to Pete Rose, baseball was the biggest reason to be alive, to Lou Piniella, and to many other designated hitters, it was, for the most part, his job.

Lou had a quick wit and liked to kid. But somehow his kidding was always aimed at Mike and his teammates and no one else. I noticed, for example, that with his wife, Anita, he seemed particularly stiff. I rarely saw him joke with her at all. I wanted to tell him to loosen up, be less distant and formal. But he and Mike were examples of ballplayers who, when all was said and done, much preferred the company of men to women. You could see this very well at parties: the guys often gathered around each other at once and began talking about the games. Wives were then all but ignored until the end of the night.

I watched Mike and Lou cavorting around the casino. They seemed so comfortable together, so sure. There's something there, I thought, that I, or any wife, can probably never achieve. The camaraderie of baseball players: it really seemed very special.

Though I enjoyed seeing Mike having a good time, I wondered also if he might be having too good a time. Tossing down hundred-dollar chips and laughing, shouting, shaking the dice—was I being silly about this or was there really something here to fear?

Trying not to be a prude, I headed for a little game of chance of my own. Mike had given me $200 earlier in the evening and joked, "Don't spend it all in one place." I'd always been intrigued by the images of baccarat—mysterious rich men in black ties with bejeweled, statuesque women—so I decided I'd give it a try. Since I didn't know how to play, I enlisted the aid of a woman I'd met on the plane. She and her husband were old hands at Vegas. They'd been here many times and knew all the ropes. Apparently she was exactly the one to ask, because within minutes I had multiplied my money several times. After only a few games, I was sitting there with $1,400.

I tipped the dealer and walked away from the table a winner. I ran and found Mike and displayed my winnings, spreading out the hundred-dollar bills like a Chinese fan.

"Who gave you those?" he asked, nervously shaking his dice. When I told him, all he did was make a loud, disgusted snort. Then he threw another round.

I stayed with him for a while and watched him lose about $300 more. I was glad at least one of us could quit these games. Finally, I said, "Are you almost ready to go up to our room?"

He threw the dice again. "No, not just yet," he said. "I think I'll play a little longer." It was 2 A.M. now, but I knew a "little longer" actually meant a lot longer.

Dejected, I took the room key from him and went up by myself.

I was not a great boxing fan and watching a big fight in person did nothing to change my mind. Two men beating each other senseless was just not my idea of a likable sport. Seeing it all up close—the blood, the splattering sweat, the jabs that sent one man's head snapping back and another's reeling to the side, the thuds and cracks of muscle against bone—I realized why I had been the only Yankee wife to come along on this trip. This fighting seemed so ridiculous.

I was also disappointed with our seats. Mike and I were sitting on the opposite side of the ring from the other Yankees. George Steinbrenner had purchased our tickets and had made certain of this. Since Mike was negotiating with other ball clubs, Steinbrenner, though still friendly in private, would not publicly allow Mike to come anywhere near. Perhaps he feared public closeness would condone Mike's disloyalty. Whatever the reason, even though Mike had pitched and won two complete World Series games for him just a month before, George treated Mike like a total outcast at this fight in Vegas.

I did enjoy the festivities right before the fight. Heavyweight boxing matches are well known for bringing out the rich and famous, like a theater opening or a gala ball. Ringside seats for a top fight can run into the hundreds of dollars per ticket, so naturally only the very well-off can afford them. Movie stars sit side by side with corporate presidents and scream for blood. Now we, too, were screaming with them.

At ringside we saw Howard Cosell standing by the press table, frowning at some sheets of paper. I wondered if he'd remember us. We'd met in Baltimore when ABC had come in '75 to telecast a *Game of the Week* from Memorial Stadium. Mike had been scheduled to pitch that game, so earlier in the day, Cosell had taken us to lunch.

"Look as pretty as you can tonight," he'd said to me. "I'm going to pan the camera over to you once or twice tonight." When the time came, though, he seemed to pan over much more than once or twice. Almost every inning, it seemed, I was a star!

"Now in the stands tonight," he said in that staccatolike speech pattern of his, "is the starting pitcher's lovely wife, the French-Canadian model, Danielle Gagnon Torrez." He'd made me feel pretty important.

This time, in Vegas, as soon as I saw him, I felt immediately warm. He'd struck me in Baltimore as an extremely gracious man, almost a father figure. He had a real knack for making his guests feel comfortable. We tried to get over to him, to say hello, but before we could, the crowd let out a huge roar. Everyone turned and jostled and stood on chairs to see what was happening.

The answer was by the arena's main door. The most famous athlete in the world was entering the room. He was Cosell's good friend, Muhammad Ali. Dressed very conservatively in a dark suit and simple open white shirt, he smiled, waved at the crowd, and shook everyone's hand like a politician just back from a landslide victory at the polls. I liked him right away. Before that, I'd always found his media image somewhat offensive—the loudmouth, the maniacal

184

braggart—but here, in person, his charm and friendly air was apparent at once. Many other celebrities in the room had found it necessary to wear sunglasses or had covered their hands with diamonds and jewels to make sure they were noticed. Ali, instead, was pure. I decided my impressions of him from the media were way off the mark.

Cosell turned back and spotted us at once. "Mr. and Mrs. Mike Torrez," he boomed. "How very nice to see you."

We shook hands and he put an arm on Mike's shoulder. "I want you to know," he said, "I was certain you would pull off those Series games back there in October. I just knew you could do it. It proves something I've been saying for a long, long time." He leaned toward Mike and said in a very low, very slow voice: "When you, Mike Torrez, are in a clutch situation, you will carry that situation to fruition each and every time. You have not proved me wrong yet."

Ali made his way through the crowd and joined us. Swarms followed him, sophisticated, dressy whites, and jazzy, cool, quiet blacks. Ali smiled warmly as Cosell introduced us.

"In particular, Muhammad," Cosell said, "I'd like you to meet Mr. Torrez's lovely wife." He put his arm around me and gently pulled me close. "And as soon as she gets rid of that big ballplayer husband of hers, I want you to know she's going to become the next Mrs. Howard Cosell."

Ali kind of flinched his eyebrows at that and gave a very mischievous grin. "This pretty lady?" he said. "Forget it, Cosell: you're much too old!"

Ali's sense of humor also came out during the fight. During the first round, he began swooping down below the apron of the ring and leering up menacingly at both fighters. But he purposely hid himself from all the cameras, until one of them, either Duane Bobick or Ken Norton, it didn't seem to matter which, landed a good punch on the other. Then Ali would leap up into the air and hoot and throw his arms high over his head. Then he came right back down almost immediately to hide once again beneath the ring. He was like a jack-in-the-box, springing up and bellowing, then retreating again. It was a pretty funny act. Much of the crowd even paid more attention to it than to the fight itself.

Once, though, when he came down, he looked over to us and almost sadly shook his head. He winced a little, as if to say, "I don't know, I may be getting a little too old for all this."

After three days in Vegas, Mike's behavior began to really get to me: he just couldn't seem to tear himself away from the crap tables. This served only to remind me of other problems.

Ballplayers often have the idea that no matter what they want, it is theirs for the taking. Even average ballplayers feel this way, since hotel bills and restaurant checks are often generously absorbed by those in charge. What scared me now was that this attitude might grow to nasty proportions as Mike's star continued to rise. When we walked into restaurants, for example, managements would now not only pick up our tab, but frequently surprise us as well with a complimentary bottle of their best wine. If we were nobility before, we were now the very focal point of the court. The prince and his princess ascending to the throne. I felt that way during the Kansan of the Year festivities, in particular. I'd sat in that convertible like the Grand Marshal of the Tournament of Roses. And I'd wondered: could all this cause Mike, or me, to begin believing we could do no wrong?

Another concern was drink. Alcohol was not something ballplayers exactly shied away from. They endorsed it on TV and quaffed it with abandon after every game. Johnny Lipon, a shortstop with Detroit in the forties and fifties, once even recalled a tavern across the street from Tiger Stadium. "Lots of the guys used to go there *before* the games," he remembered. "By the time they came out, believe me, they were pretty well gone."

Some players even drank in the *middle* of a game. In Oakland, two pitchers were each knocked out in the first innings of games of a double-header. By the time the rest of the team rolled into the locker room at the end of game two, both these pitchers were dead-drunk. They were found sprawled out semi-conscious across the tiled floor of the shower room.

Some players could handle it, of course. The most well-known of these was a third baseman with Kansas City, George Brett. In 1976, Brett led the American League in hits with 215 and batting average with .333. He would later go on to gain a lot of press attention in 1980 for his average of .390. Reaching a mark of .400 is extremely desirable since very few have ever done it in the last sixty or seventy years. The most recent to do it was Red Sox great Ted Williams, in 1941, with .406. Brett, then, was on his way to becoming one of the game's most outstanding batters.

A few years later, however, Brett and two teammates, Jamie Quirk, a young infielder, and Clint Hurdle, a loud-talking, but likable, outfielder, became well-known for something else: their home. Brett had purchased a single-family dwelling in a quiet, Kansas City suburb called Blue Springs. With Quirk and Hurdle's assistance, this house soon became notable for its constant stream of visitors and its raucous all-night parties. The Kansas City press even officially labeled it "Animal House."

Brett himself was typical of the fun-loving ballplayer. His main interest was a good time whether on or off the field. He was not one for a quiet night with a book. In fact, he once answered a reporter's question about his favorite books with the reply: "I've only read two books in my life: *Basketball Sparkplug* and *Love Story.*"

Nearly every night after home games, Brett, Quirk, and Hurdle would cruise the Kansas City area's Highway 40, playing pinball machines, chomping pizza, and looking for girls. For these three, staying out late on nights before a game quickly became second-nature.

I attributed their behavior to youth. Brett, Quirk, and Hurdle were the first to admit that they were really just living the lives of carefree bachelors. A much more real problem, I knew, was the attitude I found in many of the other players, most of them married, with entrenched habits. For them, drinking was seen as both necessary and manly, and the idea of becoming an alcoholic was never considered. Free cases of liquor were something baseball families took for granted. Fans who owned liquor companies often donated them to us or to the team. This had the effect of making at least some of the players much too dependent on alcohol. Ryne Duren, a pitcher with Philadelphia in the mid-sixties, entered an alcoholic treatment facility near the end of his career and later became an alcoholism counselor. He claimed that thirty-five percent of major league ballplayers have some kind of drinking problem. "That includes," he said, "some of those guys on Lite Beer commercials . . ."

We also knew of Kansas City catcher Darrell Porter, later with St. Louis, who also took some time off during one of the off-seasons to dry out at an Arizona treatment facility. Then, in 1982, L.A. pitcher Bob Welch wrote a book about his own experiences at the same facility. He also quoted pitcher Bo Belinsky, who more than adequately summed up the baseball drinkers' philosophy. "When I lose, I drink, and when I win"—he gave a little wink—"I celebrate!"

Las Vegas was not the first time I'd felt anxiety over Mike's carousing. During the off-season in 1975, I'd advised Mike to slow down. He loved the disco scene in Montreal, where we continued to winter, and was always racing off to a favorite

188

bar or club. He had a contract with Seagram's to do public speaking engagements, representing Seagram's at dinners and conventions. He enjoyed the work immensely. It gave his ego a great boost. But somehow I couldn't believe he was going about it the right way. I said: "I don't think Seagram's would like it if you keep spending so much time in bars, especially the same bars, your favorites. You have to be more moderate and discreet. And you can't keep neglecting new accounts."

He disagreed, said he could handle things, and continued his activities. But the following winter, for some reason, Seagram's refused to return his calls. He was finally told that they were discontinuing the line of products he'd been promoting. I was sure, though, this was not the whole truth. To me, they were also discontinuing their association with him.

He tried to act tough about it, but he couldn't keep up the facade. At one point, he just slumped into a chair and began to cry. I held his head in my arms for a while and rocked him like a little boy. It was the first time his nightclubbing activities had seriously caught up with him. It was also his first real "major league" rejection.

Another worry was drugs. With so much money now available, things could get bad. Like alcohol, baseball's very traditions foster drug use. They call it "medication" in the trainer's room, and they use it to bring down inflamed muscles and pains. Once Anna Moskau said, "These medications are fine if they take the swelling out, but I don't want Paul to end up getting stomach cancer in the bargain." Paul's father had been a semi-pro ballplayer at one time and had been given "bute tablets," or "Butazolidin," to take down inflammation. At one point, this had been a common prescription. When Paul's father died of liver cancer years later, Anna wondered if the bute tablets might in some way have been responsible.

All these medications are not necessarily harmful, of course, though the media might sometimes make it seem so. Mike Hargrove had the flu one day before a game, so his team's doctor gave him an over-the-counter antihistamine called Sudafed. But the tablets made him dizzy. After being walked in the second inning, he had to sit down on first base for a few seconds and put his head between his knees. A reporter got wind of the fact that a drug had been prescribed, and wrote a little story for the next day's news. The headline ran: "HARGROVE OD's!!" Nothing could have been further from the truth.

There have been times when drug scandals in baseball have occurred. I heard stories of team doctors dispensing amphetamines to players without prescriptions or proper examinations. Sometimes prominent players were named in these stories. More important, the idea that such things went on did not surprise me one bit. I'd been watching players gobble speed capsules for years. And amphetamines were used regularly to get a player's energy up for even insignificant games, with tranquilizers after the games to bring them back down.

Players took other drugs, too. Marijuana, some claimed, improved their playing. "I'm much more aware of what's going on out there when I'm high," one outfielder said. At parties, cocaine was sometimes as common as table salt. With new high salaries, only the highest quality was kept around. Players used it both to forget bad performances and to enhance their self-confidence for upcoming big games.

If you stayed late at a party, the host would sometimes bring out glass jars filled with all types of pills—red, green, blue, white. These jars would be plopped onto a coffee table, like a giant clear vase of M&Ms. Players then began dipping into the jar and popping the contents into their mouths.

One evening, in fact, even I succumbed. At a dinner party, I was feeling very weak and tired. "I don't know how I'll hang on," I whispered to Mike.

190

One of the players at the party suggested something small and green. "I take one of these tablets before I pitch," he said. He was reluctant, though, to give me one, as if they were intended solely for ballplayers and no one else. But I assured him I'd only indulge this once.

He handed me one of these "greenies," and I took a drink of water and washed it right down. Within a few moments I was good as new.

When Mike and I got home, though, I was still talking a mile a minute. And at 4 A.M., I was singing, dancing, skipping around the house, and polishing our silverware with meticulous joy!

Along with all these other scares, there was the one I'd been fearing all along. I kept thinking of a joke the players had been circulating and which I'd overheard one day outside the locker room:

One player asks another, "You ever talk to your wife during sex?"

The other says, "Only when I'm near a phone."

Sorry to report, I wasn't laughing. In combination with other anxieties, I began to worry about infidelity quite a lot. Since that luncheon in Baltimore years before when I'd claimed with such certainty that Mike would never cheat, a steady pressure had been building between us, causing arguments which had begun to change my mind. I'd always wanted to believe I'd given Mike no reason to cheat. But after all our tensions and disagreements I wondered if he still felt the same way.

I'd also heard a line I didn't like: "Keep the wives at home and pregnant." With a wife physically incapacitated at home, the freedom a player might then have would be all but unlimited.

I disliked, too, how players treated women in general. Reggie Jackson opened my eyes to this one night at dinner. Mike and I were with Reggie and a date at a posh New York restaurant. Reggie's date was a beautiful, blond twenty-four-year-old stewardess, but, even so, Reggie's eyes kept wandering around the room and toward the bar. Finally he leaned over to me and whispered, "Danielle, can you babysit for me for a while?" He nodded surreptitiously toward his unknowing date.

I said I would, though I wasn't sure why he asked. He got up then and went over to the bar, settling down beside a very attractive redhead. I began talking to Reggie's date, trying to divert her attention, but she kept glancing over to him at the bar, getting upset. After about a half-hour of this, Reggie came back.

"Your friend was getting pretty nervous," I whispered sternly.

He just winked. "Well, I had business," he said. Then he took up with the date as if nothing had happened.

That incident reminded me of a poem Jeanine wrote once about Reggie's ego:

> I met Reggie J. this week
> For the second or third time
> His conversation was about his Gucci tie
> Silence on my part
> How do you respond to forty-dollar ties?

Incidents like these made me see baseball players as insecure little boys, with egos as fragile as eggs. Their work was, in fact, play, which they subconsciously knew and somehow felt guilty or inadequate about, as if they were getting away with something. So, despite the assurances of thousands, even millions, they constantly needed more and more kudos from wives at home and from alluring, mysterious ladies on the road.

Many of these ladies, however, were actually young girls. In fact, they were sometimes as young as fifteen. One player once confided to me the reason why.

"These girls are usually very naive, maybe just out of high school," he said. "In many cases, they still live with their parents and they're enthralled with the idea of being with a big, famous ballplayer. The player has an expensive sports car and he dines in the city's best restaurants. He has diamond rings, beautiful clothes, large billfolds. Being with a guy like this gives a girl a lot to brag about back at the office where she works, or to her friends. And the girl's parents get into the act, too. They say, 'Hey, it looks like our little girl has finally found the right catch!'

"And if a player is married, these groupies aren't as big a risk as you might think. If a girl wants to 'blow the whistle' on a player, who's going to believe her? A well-respected thirty-five-year-old ballplayer and a silly, emotional young kid? 'Hey, I've got a wife and three children,' the player can say. 'Why would I want a young high school girl like that?' With a commitment of confidentiality from his teammates, the player's alibis are going to look pretty darn good!"

This player's comments really forced me to think: if I were in Mike's place, could I, too, resist temptation? It was an impossible question to answer. Women's feelings, I think, are much different from men's. A woman places love above all else; a man does not. I'd once asked Mike if he thought he could give up his career for his mate. He said he knew he couldn't.

"What about you?" he asked. "Could you do it?"

The question seemed stupid. I'd already done it—with him. And since joining baseball, I'd seen far too many other women do it as well. "Love is more important to us than careers," I said firmly.

Then I thought: and outside affairs.

As if all this wasn't worry enough, I looked around at my life and decided I had no friends. I went down the roster of the Yankees and realized that, in New York, I had only limited friendships: Audrey Chambliss, Dusty Zeber, Stormy Dent. Because of my illnesses, I hadn't really gotten to know any of the wives very well. Where were Jeanine, Colette, Liz, Jo? I was tired of being uprooted and constantly removed from friends and our home. I found myself praying that Mike's next move would finally provide relief.

I wondered, too, how Mike's new fame would affect the forming of friendships. If we were to really stay in one place for a while—oh, what an impossible dream that seemed!—could I form friendships outside baseball, too? With the transience of baseball friendships, I felt this was mandatory. But was it possible?

An incident before a game in Oakland had made me wonder. Liz and I had been driving toward the Coliseum, slowly weaving my powder blue Cadillac through the crowd. All at once, a short, very foul-looking man leaned over the windshield and gaped inside. Liz, in the passenger's seat, jumped back. The man gave us a menacing scowl, then let loose with some thick, scummy saliva all over the glass. For a second, I was shaken and stopped the car.

"No, no, don't stop," Liz said, "just keep driving. You mustn't let him bother you." I put my foot back on the gas and we squealed away.

Now, years later, recalling this incident, I thought: If Mike should get a new million dollar contract, would such incidents increase? And would such feelings carry over into our private life? Could I really make friends with people who might be jealous of Mike's success? And of mine?

I thought back to what other wives had said. "It can be a problem," Cindi Roberts said. "I'm often unsure if people like me because of me, or because I'm married to Leon."

And Anna Moskau said, "I'm actually very relieved when I meet someone who says, 'Oh, I'm sorry, but I really don't follow baseball at all.' It's music to my ears. I know then they will like or dislike me because of me."

Cindi's husband, Leon, in fact, often keeps his baseball career to himself. While playing with the Rangers, he once went into a Texas bank to apply for a loan. The bank clerk perused the application form, then opened his eyes wide at what Leon had written under "employer."

"Oh, Texas Rangers, huh?" He looked up like a die-hard fan. "That must be very exciting," he said. "Law enforcement's such an excellent field."

Leon quietly replied, "Yes, it certainly is."

In December, Mike signed with Boston. He'd been offered $1.5 million from New York—a quantum leap from George's original $400,000—but he and agent Gary Walker flatly said no. Twelve teams then drafted him, though only two were really acceptable. The newspapers chronicled Mike's negotiations like a tumultuous soap opera. The *Times* ran a large two-column photo of him ambling nonchalantly across now-empty Yankee Stadium, genially conversing with a groundskeeper. The image in that photo said: Mike Torrez, a super Yankee; he's done his job well. But will we keep him?

Then an article said, "Mike Torrez is seriously considering six teams: the Angels and the Padres, because he likes the weather in California, Kansas City, because of its proximity to his hometown, and Montreal, because his French wife Danielle, who comes from there, is also a model there and a TV star; also, Boston and New York because they are exciting cities and close commutes to Montreal."

The greatest paper in the world was only partly right. New York and Boston were definite possibilities, and for just those reasons. But Montreal wasn't really interested, and California

195

was like an improbable golden dream. Gary and Mike didn't seem to think Gene Autry would come up with enough money, and Ray Kroc, owner of both the San Diego Padres and the McDonald's Corporation, hung up on us when we asked for a franchise. "I don't give any of my McDonald's away to anyone for any reason!" he screamed. Also, Kansas City was out of the question. Mike had no desire whatever to return to his "homeland." He had left all that behind years before.

To me, it seemed extremely ironic that he finally signed with Boston. The Red Sox were the Yankees' chief rivals, both in '77 and for much of baseball history. But Mike always handled them well whenever he faced them. In June of '77, for example, the Sox had been clubbing home runs at a fast clip for a new team record. Carl Yastrzemski, Bernie Carbo, George Scott, Butch Hobson, Carlton Fisk—these and other Red Sox sluggers hammered thirty-three home runs in ten consecutive games. Their hot streak, though, was stopped on June 25 in New York. By guess who.

Our first visit to Boston was not very enchanting. The day was cold and dreary. Boston's buildings seemed so old and dilapidated. Fenway Park, in fact, looked so aging and grungy, I thought its rafters might collapse at the slightest boo.

It was the Bostonians themselves who changed my mind. At the signing ceremony, the press made us feel very welcome, asking Mike the usual baseball questions and me all the women's stuff.

"Where do you think you'll be living, Mrs. Torrez?" "Have you been to Boston's new shopping district yet?" "Are you proud of your husband today, Mrs. Torrez?"

Later, Mike and I mugged for the cameras. I fit a too-small Red Sox cap on his head, and we both just grinned and giggled and kidded around. Suddenly, Boston was a lot of fun.

To the question, "How do you feel about your husband's contract?," I had the obvious answer. "I feel great!" I said. The deal was for seven years and nearly three million dollars. There were bonuses, too: an extra $25,000 a year if he pitched 200 or more innings, and a no-cut clause that prohibited trades or releases without Mike's permission. Gary had done a superb job. So I thought: perhaps now our tensions can be put to rest. Mike had said early in our marriage that his goal had been a total income of $500,000. Now just three years later, he'd achieved six times that!

But even more important, there would be no more moving, no more arguments about my career. I would model part-time in Boston and Montreal and, whenever I could, take our one-year-old to Fenway Park. Mike would escape insecurity, too; no more worries and anxieties about how long he might be around. How much better things would be for us with such peace of mind!

Security, outside friendships, a happy home, resumption of my career. With so much new fame and money, if there were ever the right conditions to make all things work out, it was now. We were settling in a very "livable" American city, with a seven-year, no-cut contract and a mountain of respect. Now, our life together couldn't possibly fail!

SIX

BOSTON I

When we moved to Boston, we also decided to give up our winter residence in Montreal. We'd been staying there in the off-season every year since that first trade to Baltimore, but now, with a seven-year contract, it seemed to make much more sense that we plant roots.

The decision saddened me. One day I drove aimlessly around the suburbs of Boston trying to feel at ease. We had bought a house in Wellesley Hills—the place to be, or so we'd been told—but it just didn't feel like home. I was sure we'd made the wrong decision. I looked at the colonial houses, the Masachusetts license plates, the New England streets: could I ever like it here?

I drove back to our house. It was an exquisite gray three-bedroom contemporary ranch in a very exclusive block. One of our neighbors was the great DiMaggio's brother, Dom. He'd played for the red Sox back in the forties and early fifties. Another neighbor was the chief administrator of perhaps the most prestigious hospital in the world, Massachusetts General. Another owned a company that made fine gold components for high-tech industries.

Another neighbor was a fabulously wealthy Venezuelan from Caracas. He and his wife had purchased a five-bedroom mansion primarily for a study hall. Their children were attending a Boston university, so they, the parents, decided, what the heck, let's both go back to school ourselves. They'd temporarily left a forty-bedroom estate in Caracas, with a staff of chauffeurs, housekeepers, gardeners, and guards, and an Olympic-sized swimming pool that overlooked terraced gardens and a view of the Caribbean. They'd come straight to snobby Wellesley Hills, just one big happy family all together at a high-priced Boston school.

By comparison, our own situation was modest. They made Mike and me looked like waifs. But even so, we were doing quite well. After our impoverished backgrounds, this house we'd purchased was difficult to believe. Laid out on one level, it was L-shaped. As you drove past it, you slowly saw more and more of it, as if it was unfolding right before your eyes. It also had six bathrooms, a maid's quarters, a front door that occupied a third of the front facade, and a backyard pool. The pool's dressing cabana even matched the house! Inside, skylights, terra-cotta tiles, and floors of white polished marble and dark satin wood kept all the rooms sunny and warm.

Our kitchen was very large, twenty-three by eighteen. No countertops either, but a fully equipped butcher-block island in the middle, with spotlights throwing light from above. Shelves in the kitchen were concealed by suedelike sliding doors that hid our refrigerator, dishwasher, and storage space. A five-foot-wide skylight splashed warm sunshine over the entire room.

The pool in the back nestled to the side of a little breakfast nook. The pool itself was blasted out of ledge, and surrounding it were large containers of flowers, velvet grass, and tall evergreens. I often sat by the pool quietly in the mornings listening to the earliest birds and sipping tea. Sometimes, I'd just gaze and gaze at those hardy evergreens and wonder: have I done the right thing? Was this new life worth leavng my hometown for, my country? But I could never decide.

Money creates dilemmas. When you haven't any, you keep wishing you had a lot of it. But when actually you have a lot of it, what to do with it becomes a serious, often bewildering, concern. Our tax bracket, for example, leaped up to over seventy percent. This meant that if Mike made a gross of $400,000 a year, as his contract assured, it's conceivable he might actually bring home only $120,000! Still a sizable amount, to be sure, but in many ways not very much more than his earnings back in Oakland or even Baltimore. Tax bites in those years had been far lower. Thus, claims of multi-millionaire status could be considered somewhat off the mark.

This reality, then, made tax shelters very important. There were very normal offerings, like apartment projects and oil and gas investments. But we heard also of deals involving artwork, dairy cows, and nuclear waste! And financial "wizards" came wriggling out of woodwork to explain them all. Since the announcement of the signing of his contract, Mike had been asked to invest in all kinds of new schemes, including sporting goods, real estate, Arabian horses, a sports arena (which, if he invested, would be named after him), uniforms for youth sports teams, Montreal discos, and even rifles!

Some players had no problem with this. Reggie Jackson got three million dollars in the free agent draft and knew exactly what to do with it. He immediately began investing in cars, mainly Rolls-Royces. He also joined Gary Walker in a number of extremely smart business deals. Then he gave some of the money away for tax reasons to schools, orphanages, and youth groups.

Reggie, in fact, could be extremely generous. He enjoyed giving away money even when he didn't have to. If he took you out to dinner, for example, it was always to the finest restaurant in town. Also, now and then, when he'd sign an autograph, he'd also hand the youngster a ten-dollar bill.

"Now run along," he'd say, "and be careful how you spend it!"

Reggie, however, was not the only ballplayer I'd heard of who could handle money. The Cardinals' Pete Vuckovich, a starting pitcher later with the Brewers, collected antique furniture and invested in the restoration of historical buildings; Rusty Staub and Hall-of-Famer Stan Musial established restaurants; Preacher Roe, a pitcher in the forties and fifties, founded a supermarket; ex-shortstop Pee Wee Reese, a Dodger from the forties and fifties, became owner of a bowling alley, a storm-window franchise, and was a major stockholder in a Kentucky bank. Bev and Wes Stock were also very wise with their money: though Wes's initial major league salary had been only $7,000 (1959), Bev and Wes saved and invested so carefully that they eventually purchased a quarter-million-dollar house during the seventies in Washington State, complete with a spectacular vista of Puget Sound at their front door.

Another ballplayer who was successful with his investments, especially for one who played his entire career before the advent of free agency, was Mickey Mantle. Though initially Mantle lost a great deal of money on a restaurant deal—Mickey Mantle's Country Kitchen—he soon obtained shares in companies selling mineral water, beer, and oil wells. He also joined other famous ex-ballplayers in investing another commodity he had in abundance—his reputation. Once he was paid $3,500 just to show up at a man's birthday party. He also signed a multi-year contract with a Dallas insurance company simply to attend sales meetings and give peppy little "motivational" talks to its sales reps. This kind of opportunity was available from banks and large corporations, since the addition of a ballplayer to a board of directors, for example, was considered good publicity. In the manufacturing world particularly, ballplayers began popping up all over with endorsements: The Yankees' Joe DiMaggio (Mr. Coffee) and Phil Rizzuto (The Money Store), Boston's Carl Yastrzemski (Fenway Franks) and Ted Williams (Sears fishing gear), Kansas City's George Brett (7-Up), Baltimore's Jim Palmer (Jockey shorts), and Philadelphia's Pete Rose (Aqua Velva).

Along with this heightened visibility, there also developed a trend toward players-turned-sportscasters. The most successful of these have been NBC's Tony Kubek (once a star Yankee shortstop), Joe Garagiola (a former catcher with the Cardinals) and Bob Uecker (a catcher with the Phillies, Cardinals, and Braves). Garagiola and Uecker were particularly successful, having once been mediocre players, but using wit and charm to transform poor legacies on the field to opportunities of gold on the tube. Both wrote books, did commercials, and broadcasted games. Garagiola, for a time, even hosted the *Today Show* while Uecker can still be seen trading quips with Johnny on an occasional *Tonight Show*. The success of these two, in particular, made me realize that Mike's stature as a baseball player could and should be exploited when the time came to finally quit the game.

Even so, for Mike and me, suddenly having so much money had its ups and downs. At first, it was hard to get the hang of it. One day, for example, a man called and offered a fantastic return on a new shopping mall. "If you get in on the ground floor of this," he said, "you can grab an even bigger share than anyone else." We went for it. Mike invested close to $300,000. As the months dragged by, however, no news about the mall was forthcoming. Each time we called the man about it, he said only, "It's getting there, be patient, it's coming along. I'll get back to you." But he never did.

Finally, we'd had enough. "Listen," Mike screamed into the telephone, "there isn't any shopping center at all, is there? There never was any, was there?"

He got slippery again, so Mike hung up. The matter lingered on in the courts for years.

Mark Belanger, our friend from Baltimore, finally helped us out. He directed us to an organization Brooks Robinson had started called Professional Management Associates, or PMA. Brooks had originally proposed the idea to his lawyer, Ron Schapiro, as a way for young ballplayers with sudden high salaries to keep from losing them. Everyone in the sports world knew of fight champion Joe Louis, the famous "Brown Bomber" of the forties, dead-broke only a year or two after the end of his career. Robinson himself had lost a few thousand on a sporting goods investment after he'd retired, so he too understood how money could easily be lost.

"There are six hundred ballplayers out there who need help with their finances," he told Schapiro. Thus PMA was established, joining one other such group, Independent Management for Professionals (IMP), in Cleveland.

Mike and I joined PMA and were immediately advised on our spending. The management group then told us how to handle all our major bills, especially mortgage, utilities, and car payments. It also provided advice on new investments, giving us an excuse whenever we weren't sure. If some slick, easy-money man called us, we could say, "Well, now, this sounds very nice, but we'll have to check it out with our advisors first." If it was a bad idea, then, we'd be off the hook. "Our management group says no," we could say. "Sorry."

Financial matters thus began to straighten out gradually. Something inside me, though, would not. I wasn't sure what it

204

was, since my homesickness seemed to be lessening every day. We got around Boston more and more, and I could see it was not such a bad place. There were nightclubs, fine restaurants, museums, historical sights, and, outside the city, beautiful countryside. Whatever was bothering me, however, remained and leaped out of me one day when I was meeting with an interior decorator. Despite her fresh new designs and the excitement in her voice, for some reason I couldn't get myself fired up. I found myself not wanting to do anything too permanent. I had the unshakable feeling I wasn't going to last here the full seven years.

Sometime after the season began, I began to understand what was wrong: something about the Red Sox, something drifting out from the stories and gossip and their style. The Red Sox were a talented, some said brilliantly talented, team. They'd won only one pennant in the seventies, but they'd been contenders nearly every year. The year before, '77, a Sox outfielder, Jim Rice, had led the American League in home runs. And a Sox reliever, Bill Campbell, had had the most saves. The Red Sox also had perennial greats like veteran Carl Yastrzemski, a certain inductee into the Hall of Fame, and pitching stars Bill Lee and Luis Tiant, and booming slugger first baseman George Scott, catcher Carlton Fisk, outfielder Fred Lynn, and third baseman Butch Hobson. There were also clutch performers, like shortstop Rick Burleson and outfielder Dwight Evans. Promising newcomers were being added, too: Dennis Eckersley, a fourteen-game winner with Cleveland the year before, and Jerry Remy, the Angels' starting second baseman since 1975. Yes, and to this list could be added a big, bruising, right-handed starter named Michael Augustine Torrez.

The thing that bothered me was the Sox reputation off the field. It was well-known they had a sizable percentage of playboys. Many of these were married but kept eighteen- and nineteen-year-old girlfriends on the side. In Boston, this did not mean only road trips. One veteran was even known to have an ongoing relationship with a woman twenty years younger, while his wife, who knew the whole story, resided quietly out of state. She was content, it was said, to not make an issue of it, so as not to jeopardize the expensive tastes to which, over the years, she'd become very attached.

Another Sox playboy was stringing along three girlfriends at the same time, while his unsuspecting wife stayed home with the kids. Another had an ongoing relationship with a woman in her mid-twenties, often bringing her with him on road trips. Again, his wife had no idea. With Mike's penchant for good times and his weakness for temptation, all this, understandably, made me deeply concerned.

It was not my imagination, either. When I'd been pregnant and staying in Montreal, I once called Mike while in Detroit on a road trip. We were talking on the phone when suddenly a giggly young girl came on the line.

"Mike, Michael," she said. "Is that you, Mike? Mike?"

Mike didn't answer right away, he seemed either stumped about who it was or what to do about it. Then he said, "Who is this? Who are you? Get off the line!"

I stopped talking myself and listened.

"Mike, Mike," the voice said again. "It's me, Maureen."

Mike said he didn't know any Maureen and kept telling her to get off. I got weak as I realized she must have been connected to his room by the switchboard. For the first time since I'd been told back in Baltimore that all players fool around, I considered it might be true.

"Well, I guess it's for you," I said, disgusted, starting to hang up.

"Don't you hang up on me!" Mike snapped. Then he began yelling at this other voice, whoever she was, to get off the line.

I began to get really angry. He began complaining about hotel phone systems, how the lines must have gotten mixed up.

"Don't lie to me, honey," I said. I always called him honey when I was mad. "And I want to warn you," I said, "Don't ever let me catch you doing something you shouldn't. 'Cause I won't divorce you, you know. I'll just make your life miserable." I was mad.

The odd part about all this was that Mike had always been terribly jealous about me. He was constantly suspicious if I even said hello to another man. And he often accused me of wanting a career of my own only so I could fool around. The truth was Mike was the only man I'd ever been with in my life, and I had no temptations whatsoever to be with anyone else. I was in love with him alone. And I believed that marriage was the most sacred of trusts.

Mike was exhibiting what I'd begun to see in many other ballplayers: a feeling that he had almost a god-given right to the best of both worlds, the patient, understanding, faithful mate at home, and the wild, unchecked good time on the road.

He couldn't have both with me.

As the year went on, I saw and heard other things that in no way eased my mind. In a restroom at Fenway, a few of the wives were once chatting when a very stunning, buxom, blond bombshell came over and said she was "very good friends" with one of the outfielders. She then said she thought she'd like to introduce herself to the player's wife.

"I don't think you want to do that," I interrupted. This particular player's wife was in the stands at the time, and many months pregnant with her first child.

"But why shouldn't I?" the bombshell asked. "I'm just good friends with him. That's all!"

Mike told me later that this woman was, in fact, a lot more.

The outfielder used to pick her up on a corner near the park after a game or drop off a free ticket to her beforehand. Also, many of the other players, Mike said, had gone out with her, too. But of course, he said, this did not include him.

I heard another story about one of the infielders who got very drunk while on a road trip in New York. This was the same player who carried on with three mistresses while his wife waited innocently back home. This time, he was coming back from a night out with one of them, when their cab driver realized the girl was getting sick. The cabbie pulled over at once and the girl leaned out and retched into the gutter. Then both she and the player passed out, and the cabbie had to ask a couple of players to carry the lovebirds to their room. They were deposited on a bed, but an hour later the player woke up. He stumbled down to the lobby looking for the bar. Once there, he encountered even more trouble: not one, but both his other girlfriends had shown up to stay with him. Neither knew the other, so both had rung his room. Apparently, the player and his date had been too drunk to answer. Each of the girls then snuggled onto sofas on opposite sides of the lobby, bulging suitcases on the floor beside their feet, and settled in with paperbacks to wait.

When the player wandered into the lobby, there was no escape. He did the only thing besides baseball he knew well: acted drunk. He dashed madly through the lobby and tumbled out into the street. He then began screaming maniacally at a hooker standing on the corner. Understandably, the hooker got very frightened. She began to run. The player then started chasing her and was not seen again until just before the game the next afternoon.

Interestingly, this particular player often ended such sprees with much groaning and a head full of guilt. "I really don't know why I do these things," he'd say. "I have no business acting like this." Yet, when temptation struck again, he did the same.

In Oakland once, I had actually gotten to know one of these player's mistresses. She ran a small cosmetics shop in San Francisco, where I shopped regularly. We really hit it off.

One day she asked about my husband.

"He's a pitcher with the A's," I said proudly.

Her reaction was muted. "Oh," she said quietly, looking away. I thought this strange because normally eyes popped out of people's heads when I informed them that Mike was a pro ballplayer. Then I'd immediately be bombarded with questions. But Hillary said nothing.

Some weeks later, Liz and I were standing by a gate at the Coliseum, waiting for our tickets. Suddenly, through the crowd, I saw Hillary, her long strawberry-blond hair flipping as she hurried along. She was dressed nicely in a pale sundress with a small sash around the waist. It was as if she were trying to impress someone. When she saw me, though, she stopped, as if startled. She seemed almost sorry to have seen me.

I waved to her. "Hi!" I yelled. "I'm surprised to see you here. I didn't think you liked baseball."

I went over, but she seemed very nervous. Right away she said: "It's my first time here. I'm just meeting some friends." I invited her to bring her friends and join Liz and me in the wives' section. "There's always plenty of room," I said.

But Hillary just shook her head. "Uh, my friends really like the bleachers," she stammered. Then she made a quick good-bye, and hurried down a corridor. It occurred to me briefly that for someone who'd never been here before she seemed to have a pretty good idea of where she was going.

Months later, we were having lunch one day, and in a fit of intimacy, she revealed the truth. She'd been to Oakland Coliseum often, she said. In fact, she'd been involved with a ball-player for some time and was deeply in love.

She didn't act excited, though, so I asked the obvious question. "Is he married?" I tried to say it as delicately as possible.

She looked down at her salad. I could see the beginnings of tears at the corners of both her eyes.

"Yes," she said, "and he's not in love with me, either. He just needs someone, or something else, besides his wife. At least, that's what he tells me. I know I'm being crazy about this. But I can't seem to help myself." She kept looking down, and I noticed her long lashes brushing against her cheeks. Then, tears trickled out and down her face. She stopped speaking.

At that moment, I had two very different emotions. I wanted to wrap her in my arms and cradle her like a precious, frightened child. But I wanted also to tear her apart. What if my own husband was involved with someone like her? I was really confused at this. I seemed to care about her as if she were my sister but also hate her even worse than my lowliest enemy. It was painful for us both.

There was a part of me, too, that envied her. She got to see a side of the players that we wives never could. Our guys were in a state of much less pressure when with groupies or girlfriends. No nagging, no demands. Just fun, freedom, and the next day's game.

By the time Mike and I left Oakland, Hillary had given her player up. Mistresses, in almost all cases, play second fiddle to players' wives. Ultimately, Hillary just couldn't handle it. One day, she'd been standing in line at the Coliseum waiting for a ticket when a woman in front of her, about seven months pregnant, told the ticket man her name. Hillary nearly gasped out loud. It was her lover's wife! At that moment, she knew it must end. This woman had her lover's name, status, and future child. She also had a very definite commitment. Hillary had always known that, in the long run, she could never compete, and seeing her lover's wife in the flesh convinced her of it. After hearing about the woman for so long, seeing her that day drove the reality home.

A week later, Hillary's lover asked her to come along on his next road trip. "No," Hillary replied, "your wife is too real to me now. I don't want it anymore. There's no room for all of us in my life."

The player said, "Well, hell, you knew all along I was married. What's the big problem?"

"I knew all along," Hillary said sadly. "Yes, I knew. But I'd never been so close to her before. She's too much a part of you, a part I can never have. It's over." Hillary told me all this on one of our last days together. I was very silent as she said it, but inside I leaped with joy. That's one less of them out there, I thought. I didn't like the idea of attractive women getting all hung up on men like my husband. And I didn't like the idea of our men taking advantage of the situation.

But I was learning, too, that, no matter what I liked, this was exactly how it all worked.

One would expect that so much philandering would make baseball players sexually sophisticated and wise. But nothing seemed farther from the truth. Through the years I'd heard stories of players telling their wives they'd gotten crab lice from the "team laundry basket" or of players having contests by measuring their private parts. There was also the relief pitcher on the Yankees who couldn't unwind after an important game without making love to his wife in their kitchen sink! And the couple in Baltimore who'd devised a new method of fertilization.

"Right after we make love," this player said, "my wife gets down on the floor and stands on her head. We're hoping it will make enough sperm come down and get something going."

This sexual ineptitude derived in great part from the players' mystique. Ballplayers are looked up to as being "real men." They do all physical things very well. Certainly they know a lot about sex.

This, of course, makes many of them, even if they don't have the slightest idea what they're doing, too proud to ask. And with the ease with which sex is available to them, there's no pressure ever to change. So, if they form bad habits early in life, they never have reason, or the demands, to change them.

It was Montreal, in fact, where a player's wife first confided to me that her husband was a lousy lover. The husband was a relief pitcher with the Expos, and one day his wife began complaining out loud. This started off innocently enough, only picky little things like everyone feels when the day isn't quite working out the way you planned. Before long, though, she was off on a tear.

"It wouldn't be so bad if he didn't just lie there," she said. "I'm so tired of doing all the work! It just seems I'm always having sex with him without anybody making love to me."

As the years went on, I'd find out how amazing it was for the wife of a ballplayer to say anything at all about sex. It was just not done. When it did happen, however, we noted that the game had a very definite effect on this aspect of our lives. After a tough loss, for example, many players had difficulty going to bed at all. Mike was one of these, and he'd sometimes stay up half the night watching TV, having a drink or two, pacing back and forth around the house. The idea was to bring down his adrenaline. So, on nights like these, going to bed or generously making love was all but impossible.

On the mound in 1978, Mike tried very hard. He was stung repeatedly by the comments in the press and in the stands, things like, "With all that dough, does he really care if he wins or loses?" Or, "Twenty-five grand just for walking to the

212

mound." But he cared. In fact, he cared a lot. And more important, he was determined to prove it.

The season started, as it always does for him, very slowly. He just couldn't seem to get going. But late in May, he found his groove. He started popping fastballs and curves like a mind reader. He seemed to know exactly what each hitter couldn't take. Then later in July, for some reason, the formula fell apart.

The Sox were having a good year in '78, so Mike should have been, too. At midsummer, they were twelve games ahead. I was very scared of New York, though, since I knew what they could do. I'd seen them up close, after all, only a year before. But Mike couldn't do a thing to stop them. He ended up beating the Yankees only once the whole year. Former teammate Sparky Lyle would later say he never considered Mike that good anyway. He'd simply been lucky, especially playing a year with the Yankees.

To Mike, his slump was baffling. Where last year's pennant drive had seen him shine, this year he could do nothing right at all. He walked around helplessly in the locker room trying to explain it to reporters. "I have never been through something like this," he told a man from the *Boston Globe*. "I'd like to say something more about it, but I just don't know what it would be . . . all I know is I'm trying . . . I am trying as hard as I've ever tried . . ."

But no matter what he tried, he just couldn't win. Forty days and forty nights it went on. About eight or ten games. He could not win one.

I felt bad about it all, but I was glad at least that I wasn't the cause. At least I didn't think I was. There was a constant tension in our lives now, an underlying feeling that we were heading in opposite directions. His love for the fast and flashy, mine for something more sedate and domestic. But even these feelings were thin and cloudy. I just hoped and wished and prayed for him. And waited with the rest of Boston for his slump to end. As one writer said, "Mike Torrez is not a loser. He just can't stop losing."

Without Mike's help, the Sox began a slow but steady nosedive. Where they had been leading fourth-place New York by as many as fourteen games back in July, by the end of September that lead had totally disappeared. In the final week of the season, it was the Yankees who led the pack.

With a huge sigh of relief, then, I watched the Sox regain control in the last few days. On September 29, Mike pitched both himself and Boston out of this rut, by shutting out the Tigers, 1–0. Low curves, change-ups, fastballs, slick sliders— everything came smoothly together. Only three Tiger batters managed a hit. Mike Torrez had returned.

The regular season ended with New York and Boston tied for first place. Thus on October 2, the two teams met at Fenway for only the second one-game playoff in the league's history. And Mike would be pitching.

Yankee–Red Sox end-of-season games are classic. I once heard about Babe Ruth playing outfield all season for the Yankees, then coming in to pitch in a late 1933 game, and beating the Red Sox 6–5. In years following, at least two pennants would be decided on October days between New York and Boston. Also, that famous sixty-first home run given up by Red Sox pitcher Tracy Stallard to Roger Maris took place in October. Yes, late-season Yankee–Boston games were hard to forget.

This game, too, had all the trappings of the World Series. People had come up from New York wearing Yankee jackets, waving pennants, and sporting T-shirts that read, "Boston sucks." Boston retaliated with chants and banners saying, "Yankees, go home" or "Let's go, Yaz." Kids clambered up billboards and adjoining buildings and peered down for a free view. And outside, people poured from Boston's subway and the parking lot to converge at the main gates. It was indeed a big day.

For six innings, Mike held the Yankees off. Their entire lineup connected only twice for base hits. The rest were weak grounders, fly balls, and pop-ups to the infield. I was terrified the whole game. I kept looking over at the Yankee wives, thinking, "I wish I were sitting with them." I knew what it meant to win, and I'd become very unaccustomed to anything less. Before the game, I saw George Steinbrenner in the stands, and he said, "There are really no winners or losers, Danielle. But someone must be best." Immediately I'd thought: but will it be Boston?

Early in the game, Reggie Jackson stepped to the plate. I wanted to hide behind my seat. He swung with that huge falling-away swing of his, and the ball hurtled toward the left-field wall. I relaxed as Jim Rice settled on the warning track and caught it for an easy out.

As other Yankees came to bat, I marveled at how one's allegiance affects one's judgment. Some of these Yankees never struck me as particularly great players, though certainly almost all were very good. When, as a Yankee, I'd wanted them to get a base hit, many times they wouldn't. Then, I'd wanted them to hit it out of the park every time. Since they couldn't, I'd lose faith in their ability. Now, seeing them as the opposition, they were killers, every one of them. I assumed that each could hit a mile-high homer any time he liked.

In the seventh, Boston was still ahead, 2–0. If Mike could just hang on for three innings more, we would make it. After one out, though, things went awry. Chris Chambliss stepped to the batter's box and, once again, I was scared stiff. "Surely he'll get a hit," I thought. This time, I was right.

Then Roy White, the left fielder, came up. White's average was only fair, but I knew that in the clutch, this meant nothing. I felt certain he'd get a hit, too. Once again, I was right on the money.

The next batter, Jim Spencer, flied to left field. That made two outs, so, any kind of weak connection could now end the inning. There were two players on, but the Yanks were still behind, two to zip. Despite any problems with Mike or being homesick for Montreal or fearful of the players' fooling around, I knew how the game was played. The wives' game, that is. I was with the Red Sox now, and it was pennant time: no room today for misplaced loyalties. Boston must win.

Up stepped Bucky Dent. With many of the rest of Boston's fans, I secretly breathed a sigh of relief. Bucky was by no means a powerful or consistent hitter. He'd managed only .247 the year before, and was batting slightly lower this year. In fact, in situations like this, a manager would not hesitate to pinch-hit for him. He might come through, but he sure as hell wouldn't hit it hard. Bucky hit three, maybe four home runs a year. He was also not that terrific in the clutch. Mike would blow three fast ones by him and stride triumphantly off the mound. Thank God, I thought: Bucky Dent.

Mike peeked at the runner on first, then glanced to second. Then he cocked back and threw. It was a curve but it broke too far to the left. Ball one.

Mike glanced at the runners again, then leaned back once more. His fastball blazed right for the plate, though slightly inside. Bucky swung. The ball clopped straight down and ricocheted off his foot. Foul ball. This latest pitch had done the trick.

Bucky tripped backward out of the box, wincing in pain. The Yankee trainer came running out and gave Bucky's foot a quick examination. Then the batboy came out and inexplicably switched bats. Later, Mickey Rivers said he had requested it. Rivers, in the on-deck circle, had wanted that particular bat, a favorite of his, for himself. It was old and chipped, and, he thought, full of luck. Bucky had grabbed it without thinking, and Rivers had had it switched.

Bucky reached over and picked up the new bat, then cautiously stepped back to the plate. I looked at his low batting stance. Stormy had once advised him to stand just that way, bending real low at the plate. Bucky dismissed the idea, just as Mike had dismissed my own suggestion about his windup years before. But, as with Mike, Bucky's coach had later advised him to do exactly as his wife had proposed. He'd been using that low, stooped stance ever since.

The sun was low now, as the shadows began darkening the grass in left field. I pulled my coat collar snug. A few stray candy wrappers swirled around me in the nippy air. I looked at Mike, standing tall and calm, not seeming cold at all.

Inside, I knew, he had to be nervous. This inning could make or break him. He'd won sixteen games this year, but not one counted more than this. Mike was a major star, he'd been around the big leagues for quite a long time, and, as everyone in the park knew, he could do the job. But he was still being asked to prove it. Today's game meant everything.

But what was I worrying about? This man at the plate was like a sweet farm boy from Georgia. In many ways, he was just a babe. Very confidently, Mike checked the runners again, then gracefully drew his big arm behind his head. Then he flung with all he had toward the plate. It hurtled as if shot from a cannon, another masterful stroke. Again, like the second pitch, it whipped along maybe a tad too inside and maybe a little high this time as well. But it was fast, a rough pitch to see. If Bucky tried for it, I was sure he'd miss. The entire park, in fact, seemed to feel the same way, because almost all 40,000 leaned back and relaxed. Mike Torrez and Bucky Dent. The champion vs. the kid. It was not much of a contest.

Bucky hauled back and swung. More surprisingly, he connected. The ball sailed smoothly upward toward Fenway's short left field. Everyone almost nonchalantly straightened up to watch. Mike stood on the mound watching, too. As soon as it was hit, though, I marked "F-7" in my scorebook. Easy fly ball for Carl Yastrzemski. The inning, I thought, was over.

Bucky's clout, though, kept rising. Higher and higher it went, heading frighteningly toward the top of the wall. Mike stood at attention watching it go. Carlton Fisk, too, stood up and took off his face mask and stared into space. Suddenly, everyone in the park knew the ball might actually leave the park. It was heading straight for the top of the wall!

The next thing we knew it was picking up speed. It seemed even to jump up suddenly, as if propelled by some invisible, diabolical Yankee gust of wind. It then went clattering into the screen high over left field. Bucky jogged around the bases, grinning from ear to ear, as his teammates and the visiting fans went wild. He skipped up to the plate and stomped on it triumphantly with both feet. What we'd all assumed was not possible had just happened. Bucky Dent had hit one out.

The wives in the Yankee section exploded. I could see them clapping, hugging, dancing up the aisles. I flashed quickly on a year ago this very month. New York was now winning, 3–2.

In the eighth, Reggie Jackson put it away. He hit a home run into the bleachers. An inning later, there was nothing left to deny. The Yankees finally won, 5–4. Mike, his new team, and I as well, had lost the game. I now knew how it felt.

On the drive home from the park, Mike was quiet. The mood in the locker room, he said, had been like a funeral. No one had said anything negative—players understand these things happen, and can happen to any one of them—but he'd still felt as though he'd let them all down.

Back home, he pulled out an expensive bottle of Scotch. I grabbed a glass and joined him. Tonight, I'd drink, too. He turned on the Betamax, and we watched the game. Through six innings Mike said nothing, just kept drinking and staring at the set. Then came the seventh and Bucky Dent.

Mike leaned forward and watched himself wind up, turn, and thrust forward his arm. As the ball reached the plate, Bucky swung with precision, and Mike's pitch took off at once, a steady climb at forty-five degrees, a now unmistakable home run. The camera focused in, almost cruelly, as the ball smashed into the chain-link fencing above the left-field wall. "Home run, Bucky Dent!" cried the announcer.

Mike rolled his eyes upward and shook his head. He still couldn't believe it.

"Damn," he said softly, the only word he could find.

He looked down at his drink and then at his right arm. For a minute or so, holding each other very hard, we cried.

Nineteen seventy-nine began with renewed doubts about winners and losers. Despite the security of Mike's seven-year contract, I really began thinking, after we'd lost the playoff, about how quickly things can change, turn around, even end. And without the slightest warning.

The year before, in Winter Haven, at our first spring training with the Red Sox, Mike and I got friendly with one of the Sox infielders, a long-time veteran named Tommy Helms, and with his wife, Rita. I spent a lot of time with Rita at the Winter Haven Holiday Inn, where we all stayed. Tommy and Rita had two boys, always running in and out and playing in the pool and rec room.

It was around Easter time, too, and on Easter Sunday we hid eggs for the players' children all over the hotel grounds. I was used to Easter in Florida by now, after so many spring trainings. Usually, though, it was just wives and kids, as the players occupied themselves with practice down at the field.

One day, Rita was helping me tint my hair. We were in her

room looking out toward the pool. Suddenly, Tommy emerged from across the way and started walking toward us. But he wasn't supposed to be here. He was supposed to be back at the park with the rest of the guys.

"Rita," I said, "what's wrong with Tommy? Why isn't he at the park?"

I couldn't see Rita's face, but I could hear her gasp. Tommy and Rita had been dreading this day for years. They'd been trying to prepare for it, financially and emotionally, but now, all at once, here it was. I looked at Tommy, afraid to turn back to Rita. She was extremely tense. Her fingers were digging into my shoulders.

Kind of mindlessly, Tommy went to the refrigerator and pulled out a beer. Rita said nothing.

"I'm going to go get a haircut," Tommy said, as if not knowing what else to say or to do. Then he left the room.

Tommy was close to age forty. He could have expected, at best, only one or two more active years. He'd been with two teams, in fact, the year before, 1977, and neither had let him play many games. Fortunately, he had a business venture on the side, so he and Rita didn't need to worry all that much about making ends meet. But even so, the end of baseball hit them like a brick. He had been released.

Rita turned from me and walked around the room. They had a cramped little two-bedroom, with bunkbeds for the kids, makeshift racks of clothes, and things like toasters and irons on the dresser or the floor. During spring training, this was how we all lived.

"You know, Danielle," she said slowly, "no matter how much you prepare for this day, no matter how much you get ready, it's still so hard. It's like waiting for death. We all know it's coming. But we're never ready."

I felt a sharp stabbing pain in my stomach as I realized, even with the security of long-term contracts like Mike's, everyone in baseball lived on borrowed time. There are only so many pitches in an arm, so many miles in a pair of legs. Rita sank to the edge of her bed and stared at the floor. It was over: all she and Tommy had known for nearly twenty years was today, on this bright sunny Florida morning, suddenly gone. I put my arms around her, and we sat together saying nothing for a very long time. Then, we sipped tea in my room with Linda Fisk, Sue Evans, and Dede Lynn. It was like sitting with a widow at her husband's wake. It was helpful for her that we simply be there.

That incident, for the first time, forced me to face how tough it would be to leave this game. In some manner, it put its hooks in you. You didn't get out all that easily. You lived in a hovel every spring training, you put up with loneliness during the season, abusive fans, tormenting anxieties, and a continual rootlessness. But despite it all, it was impossible even to imagine anything else.

I remembered other stories about leaving, some I'd seen, many I'd heard. The year before, 1977, I'd been told of a night when Dave Giusti had been pitching for Oakland, while his wife, Virginia, watched from the stands wringing her hands. It was obvious to everyone in the league that the end for Dave was near. He'd been a star pitcher for fifteen years with teams like Houston and Pittsburgh, but now all his youthful stuff was gone. Would this night in 1977 be his last performance? Could he make it even to the end of the season?

As she watched him struggle on the field, Virginia Giusti kept twisting her fingers around and occasionally trying to light a cigarette. Her hands shook violently, as she picked up a match. I'd never heard of such nervousness before. The idea frightened me.

Bev Stock and Connie Robinson also told me of their last days. At least, Wes and Brooks had gone out in style. Kansas City had honored Wes with an award presentation before his

221

final game, and Brooks had been honored with Brooks Robinson Day. For both wives, though, these were extremely sad affairs. Connie remembers standing on the field with Brooks and their four children and looking up into the grandstands at 50,000 sobbing fans. She cried, too, right there on the field, especially when she realized what this final day at Memorial Stadium actually meant. It was the end of wild applause, high drama, the lure of pennants. The beginnings of it all every spring, the heart of the beast under hot summer suns, and the final tensions with September's chill.

"I went to nearly every game of Brooks's career," she said. "And yet all I could feel that day was regret over the few I'd missed." And that she could never make them up.

Jeanine Duncan had also found baseball rough to leave. Loneliness from road trips had given her agony. She looked forward to the day when she could wake up each morning with Dave beside her in their bed. But when that time finally came, it was not long before she realized it could never work out. Dave grew far too sullen without the game.

After a year of trying, Jeanine encouraged Dave to go back. He soon took a job with the Cleveland Indians as their pitching coach and once again was himself. It meant even more time away from her than before, but by now at least she knew the truth. Baseball was something Dave simply could not do without.

In Boston, I saw other players with the same problem. Carl Yastrzemski was one. Though in his late thirties, he still moved like a quick and competent young boy. The reason for this was that he took his preparations for the game very seriously. He worked out regularly during the off-season—many players did not—and during the season he made certain he was well-rested and never played with an injury. Mike said Yaz was driven: he had been with the Red Sox since his rookie year of 1961, and, in the eighteen years since, the Sox had won two pennants, but never a Series. Yaz wanted to win a World Series just once before he retired, so he stayed in the game and did whatever he could, playing outfield or first base or serving as the designated hitter. He was the Rock of the Red Sox, a quiet, affable father-figure, a cooperative, skillful sage. Because he took the game and his position in it so seriously, he still belonged.

But one of the Sox starting pitchers, Luis Tiant, was another story. Luis was big and fat and, at his claimed age of thirty-eight, a year older than Tommy Helms. He looked, however, about ten years older. I'd look at his worn face and his sagging muscles and wonder, why does he stay in year after year? Isn't this a game for young men and boys? Why doesn't he get out?

I never asked him, of course, but I knew one thing: I didn't want Mike to do the same. The incident with Tommy and Rita had made me think. Maybe Luis didn't get out because he didn't know how. Perhaps he had no idea what else to do. My own husband, it seemed, had the same problem.

During many off-seasons I'd pushed Mike to develop new interests. Like the other players I'd heard about, the smart ones, I wanted him to start building something for his life after baseball. From the other examples, it was obvious that he'd best do this while his name still spelled success. A Mexican restaurant perhaps? Some kind of concession at Fenway Park? But though he agreed with me, all he ever ended up doing during the winter were occasional speaking engagements, a few radio talk shows, or lunch with his lawyer. Also, without fail, he visited discos at least once a week with a few of his buddies. Disco Mike, the fans in Boston began to call him. Then, before he knew it, winter was over and we were back in Florida for spring training. It was as if his calling in life was to be a carefree superstar, to just have a good time. He refused to consider that someday it would end.

Now that we had a son, Mike's carelessness about the end of his baseball career became intolerable. It was one thing to live wild and free when it was just the two of us, but now we had Iannick's future to consider, too. How secure would it be if his daddy took such a lackadaisical attitude toward his own?

Making matters worse, 1979 was not a good one for Mike on the mound. If he had been trying hard to prove himself the year before, that he wasn't just in it for the money, that he had his pride, he now had to redeem himself for that catastrophic gopher ball to Bucky Dent. The fans and the press remembered all.

Though the year began well enough, with the Sox in contention through the first half, a collapse again crippled both Mike and the team toward the season's end. After August 7, in fact, Mike won only three games. And he ended the season by leading the American League in walks with 121, in runs allowed with 144, and with an extremely disappointing ERA of 4.50. The only good thing about '79 was that our old teammates, the Orioles, won the division. I could be happy, at least, for Kenny and Colette.

I wondered how much the players' carousing had affected their collapse. Red Sox playboys: I kept turning the phrase over and over in my mind. I got into a confidential conversation with a newspaper reporter one afternoon. What this reporter revealed to me bothered me more.

There were women, lots of them, and not all teenagers. Many were classy, upwardly mobile professionals—lawyers, bank executives, vice presidents of small corporations. There were two in particular, he said, who made a hobby of chasing star players. They went to all the games, attended all the parties, and very slickly and intelligently plotted their way to players' beds. They'd set their sights on someone and just

224

zeroed in. If the player was at all inclined, they'd bag him. Their percentage, the reporter claimed, was extremely good.

I didn't know if Mike was involved in any of this, but I did know that lately I'd been getting awfully suspicious. He was coming home at night later and later, sometimes just before dawn. And on the road, I'd often call his room at all hours and he wouldn't be there at all.

One night, it all overflowed. Mike was in New York on a road trip while I was home in Boston. At a quarter to five one morning, the phone rang. It was Mike.

He started babbling about Reggie Jackson and Studio 54. What a great time they'd just had, he said. I guessed he must have just gotten in. Then he wanted to speak to Iannick and started demanding I put him on the phone.

"Of course I won't put him on," I said. "He's a baby. And he's fast asleep."

Mike started babbling again. "Do you love me?" he said. "Do you?" Before I could say a word, he added almost harshly, "Well, it doesn't matter, I love you anyway." Then he hung up.

A change had taken place. It just wasn't the same since when we'd first met. There was a hard edge to his voice now. Something missing, but something had been added, too—an undertone of sarcasm, impatience . . . bitterness. Tender intentions, it seemed, had disappeared completely.

I thought about the insults and the fights. By now, Mike's going away on road trips was a great relief. Where once I had been lonely and sad about this time away, now I saw these trips as mini-vacations. I'd take nice warm baths and quietly read myself to sleep. No arguments, no harsh demands. It had reached the point where looks of disgust from both of us had replaced looks of love. I'd even started taking sleeping pills so

225

I'd be too tired to deal with him between the sheets. It was not a nice life.

Our fights covered a wide range. I wanted him to stay home more in the evenings, to stop partying so much, to drink less and to start thinking about a second career. In turn, he wanted me to spend more time with Iannick and be at home in the daytime more often, despite the fact we now employed a nanny. He wanted me also to forget about modeling. He kept accusing me, in fact, of only wanting a career so I could get involved with other men.

"I don't care about other men," I'd yell. "I just want my husband, my son's father!" These particular accusations wounded me more than any other.

Near the end of '79, Mike became extremely upset over a partnership I'd formed with two Boston photographers. Our goal was a very fashionable approach to advertising for large hotels and exclusive clubs. Mike attacked the idea by saying, "Why would someone want to hire you for an important job like that?" Then he added, "Why can't you just stay home and take care of our son? Why can't you be more like Allen Hobson?"

Allen Hobson was third baseman Butch Hobson's wife. She was a pleasant, serene woman and I liked her a lot. A pretty Alabaman, she was extremely homespun: she cared only to stay out of the limelight and take care of her two daughters.

It was very pleasant to watch Allen and her girls. I knew, however, I could not be just like her. Sure, I wanted to handle my own child as smoothly as Allen handled hers. But to Allen, being an excellent wife and mother seemed achievement enough. Try as I might, I couldn't seem to fit the same mold. Baking cookies and reading to my children went only so far. I needed more, some greater challenge, some wider goals.

226

Many women seemed to reach their peak with domesticity. For some reason, I could not.

I began comparing myself to other Boston wives, too. Pitcher Bill Lee's wife Mary Lou, for example, had always let her husband's antics slide right off her back. If Bill had been my husband, I know I'd have been too embarrassed to leave the house. He was called "Spaceman" in those days and he used to do all kinds of unorthodox things, like wearing shorts during batting practice, taking a trip to Red China, and jogging the five miles or so from his home to the park, rather than driving a Cadillac or sports car like most of his teammates.

He also held impromptu press conferences at his locker and told the press anything that came into his mind. During the '75 World Series, he predicted that a combination of pyramid power plus a full moon the night of the final game would win it for the Sox. (It didn't!) Another time he explained how he loved pancakes topped with flakes of marijuana. For this one, Bowie Kuhn, the Commissioner of Baseball, fined him $250.

Mary Lou, in contrast, was like his guardian angel. I always had the feeling she knew something more, like a wise old mind in a pretty young body. She had originally been a schoolteacher in her home state of Alaska, and her job now seemed similar: she'd pull Bill back when he got too far out of control. She was steady and rational while he was erratic and silly. This balance seemed to make their marriage work.

As much as Mike and baseball had become a huge chunk of me, I couldn't do the same. I couldn't spend my life much longer just planning everything around his "game," and carefully considering and protecting him at the cost of my own interests. I knew, also, that if somehow things ever fell completely apart, I didn't want to end up like so many other wives, who, upon divorce or separation, had nothing else

227

around them to fill the gap. "When you divorce baseball," I remembered someone once said, "baseball divorces you."

I had seen this happen with the wife of one of the Sox relievers. She had been a very vibrant mate, always rooting like mad from the stands and attending gatherings and banquets by her husband's side. But one day she was nowhere to be found. I asked one of the wives what had happened to her.

"Oh, you haven't heard?" someone said. "She's getting a divorce. She won't be coming at all any more."

And this was just how it happened: none of us ever saw her again. It was as if she'd been condemned to some unknown oblivion. Very simply, she just disappeared.

SEVEN
BOSTON II

During the next six months, things reached a point of no return with Mike. Every night, I cried myself to sleep, and days were little more than a wearying string of disagreements and looks of reproach from us both. How much longer could it last?

I decided to lose myself in work. I began by winning a major modeling assignment, my first big one since I married Mike. A brochure was being shot in Jamaica. I also got involved with putting together a flashy brochure for a major hotel in Montreal. Both assignments took me away from home for days at a time. Mike was far from pleased.

Finally, my career and Mike's feelings clashed in public. I'd been asked to host a TV show called "Disco Dazzler," a fund-raiser for a Boston PBS TV station. It would be a live six-hour program, direct from a huge Boston disco.

I interviewed many guests—international TV and rock stars, politicians, socialites—and had great fun. It was just like ten years before with *Pop* in Montreal. But about mid-

229

night, I ran out of people to interview. Since Mike was there, I pulled him in front of the camera and tried to wing it.

At first, I didn't know what to ask. I just knew we needed someone and that my husband was one of the biggest celebrities in town. So I asked him about the obvious. Discos.

"Mike, you travel a lot," I began, a little awkwardly. "You've seen many discos around the country. How do you rate the discos in Boston?"

Mike looked at me like I was crazy, then darted his eyes from side to side. Within seconds, he looked terrified. But why? He was certainly used to the press and to TV cameras by now.

He blurted out some kind of answer, then wiped his brow. I didn't know why he was acting so scared, but there was no doubt for anyone, including viewers at home, that he was. As the interview continued, I watched him wipe his brow nine times more—after every question!

Later, he admitted he'd feared the questioning might be some kind of trick. Had I been trying to embarrass him or accuse him or trap him into revealing something on camera?

By now, my close friends had become extremely tired of hearing the same old problems. One finally looked at me directly and said, "What about divorce?" Then she added, "It seems to me there are only three alternatives: you can go on as you have; you can try to change him; or you can divorce."

I lowered my head, looked down at my wedding bands. I knew things couldn't go on like this, I had really reached my limit. I needed to be more than just Mrs. Mike Torrez. I couldn't be happy staying home the rest of my life, being only his wife and nothing more. It just wasn't me.

Trying to change him was impossible. Everything I said was now met with scorn. I no longer believed either of us could change. We were both pretty stubborn and we wanted what we wanted. Divorce, it seemed, was probably the only answer.

But it wouldn't be as easy as all that. It was true that I hated what Mike seemed to crave: discos, careless spending, playboy friends. But strangely, I still loved him. I hated the things he did. But I still couldn't stop caring for the man.

Daisy's was the final straw. Driving in Boston one night, I saw Mike's shining brown 450 SEL double-parked at a busy corner. I pulled up behind and looked across the sidewalk. Daisy's. It was a bar where Mike so often went for a quick one with the boys. He'd described the place as a staid, boring men's pub, a quaint hangout where he just talked sports with other guys. But as I sat in my car staring at it, I watched young girls streaming in and out. It was obviously not what he'd said.

I went inside. The place was colorful and noisy and packed with people. Three bartenders bustled behind the bar, with massive blowups of old movie posters and black-and-white glossies of Boston athletes on the walls. Tiffany lamps, video games, beefy young doormen in soccer shirts. There was a shimmering stained glass partition separating the bar from the couples on dates having dinner. The Village People wailed on a sound system overhead, while a basketball game buzzed on a small TV at the end of the bar. And girls—young, vibrant, pretty, available. Some men's club.

I stood in the entryway and surveyed the room. There were faces all over this place I knew. The Detroit Tigers were in town to play Boston, and many of them were here talking to these pretty young girls. There were Red Sox here, too, many of whom Mike and I had had at our house for dinner or parties. And the faces I saw, on either team, I knew were married.

231

Standing to my right, however, was the only player in Daisy's I knew was single: longtime veteran Rusty Staub. Staub had played with many teams at many positions over a period of twenty years. He knew us very well. I looked over to him, and he merely looked back, then glanced toward Mike. My husband was standing a few feet away, his back to me, a young girl's arms draped around one of his. The young girl saw me first, then the other players saw me, too. Suddenly, everyone stopped moving. The bar itself got very still then, and, for a few moments, only the play-by-play on the TV could be heard. I had broken Daisy's most ironclad rule: no players' wives.

The girl standing with Mike let go of him as soon as she saw me. Then her purple blush deepened as she looked at me with total fear. She had guessed who I was.

Mike looked at her, then did a few double-takes at everyone else. Very slowly, he turned and saw me. His face immediately drained of color. Then his jaw tightened and his neck muscles got very thick. He was upset, he was angry. I had violated his sanctuary. I had caught him in the act. And his friends, too.

He rushed up to me, grabbed me by the arm. "Let's get out of here," he said. But I refused to go. I was not trailing behind him anymore. I was going to stay at Daisy's for a while and take a long, good look.

I looked every player in the place straight in the eye. I wished I could beam all the wives in both leagues to this very spot. "C'mon girls," I wanted to say, "let's all have a look." There was no longer any doubt in my own mind that what I'd been told so many years ago was true.

"Don't kid yourself," the wife had said, "all the guys do it. Including Mike." It was now undeniable.

Suddenly, on the sound system overhead, came a hit song of that year, "Another One Bites the Dust," by Queen. Mike and I, it told me, had come finally to our end.

232

In May of 1980, I visited Fenway Park for the last time. I rarely came early enough for batting practice anymore (usually two hours before a game), but today was different. I'd been to a lawyer's office and had come over to the park directly afterward. It would be my last chance to see Mike for a long while. I'd been meeting with a divorce lawyer for many weeks, and he'd devised a plan. Mike had joked in the past that if I ever divorced him, I'd have to find him in order to serve the papers. My lawyer advised that I keep everything secret. The papers would be handed to Mike while he was on the road. Since he'd be leaving for a road trip after tonight's game, the plan would be executed within a couple of days. I was still riddled with doubt, still upset about actually having to end my marriage once and for all. But I forced my fears below. I had to do this, had to go through with it.

I looked out at the bright ballfield. All these fully grown men scampering around in odd white suits and visored caps. I thought of how they'd once been cute little boys. I remembered a day outside Yankee Stadium. Mike and I were in our Cadillac and carefully squeaking through one of those crazy mob scenes. Suddenly, Mike stopped the car.

"What's wrong?" I asked.

He didn't answer. I saw a skinny boy with dark hair staring intently, hopelessly, at each passing car. He was praying, I knew, for an autograph. He strained forward while his mother crossed her arms over his chest and held him close. The two of them looked lost and out of place, like Mike the night I'd met him. Then the kid saw Mike beckoning to him. His child's eyes and mouth opened wide with delight. He leaped toward us, not even glancing toward the oncoming cars. Mike grinned at him and opened his window, though just a crack. Other hands, other arms, were pushing at the car all the way around. Behind us, horns honked like mad. Mike ignored it all and took the crumpled program from the boy's hands. The child's fingers, with bitten nails, curled around the inside of the window, brown eyes watched intently as Mike signed a page and passed it back. The boy lit up wildly but then ducked his head shyly as Mike smiled back.

Mike said something to him in Spanish, then rolled up his window. He gave me a quick, embarrassed look, then sat up very straight and drove on without looking at me again. It was as though he were telling me: "All right, I did it. I stopped for a kid, but I don't want to talk about it. Just don't say anything."

I was so proud of him that day, very grateful he could perform such a kind act. But I wondered also how healthy it was for a young boy to grow up around so much adulation, both seeing it and perhaps wanting it one day for himself. Did I want Iannick, for example, following his daddy's footsteps? There was so much good about this game, but so much bad that came with it.

I looked at the rafters of Fenway Park. This place had seemed so crumbly when we'd first come here two years before. Tonight, however, I felt a funny, nostalgic warmth. It was like leaving an old friend. I would really miss this old park, and all the other parks, too. I knew, though, I'd never really be welcome here again. Like other wives who had "divorced baseball," I was about to disappear. I would no longer be a part of this team. I would no longer be Mike Torrez's wife.

I watched Mike doing his usual sprints from left to right field. Then he walked and chatted for a while with Dennis Eckersley. Then once again, sprinted. I watched him as I had watched him many times before. He was drenched with perspiration, the towel around his neck heavy and limp and not much help. Then he spotted me sitting with Susan, my housekeeper, and with Iannick, who was unimpressed and busy with a stuffed animal. From way across the field, Mike's great smile contrasted sharply with his dark, sunburnt face. Suddenly, he began trotting towards us, avoiding in the process a player, a line drive, and a TV camera.

He was spied by a ten-year-old boy who clutched a baseball. The boy ran toward the railing as a crowd gathered and pleaded with Mike for autographs. I made my way through them, and Mike pulled me against him, hard, and smacked me on the cheek. Then he picked up our son and disappeared into the dugout.

Back at my seat, I saw the ten-year-old boy again, now darting up my aisle. With big strides, he climbed two steps at a time, losing his balance as he reached me, then tripping and landing right in my lap. We both broke out laughing as I helped him to his feet.

"Mrs. Torrez," he said, "please sign my ball?" I looked down at his dirty ball, held so preciously and tightly by tiny fingers. There were a few scribbles on the ball near traces of scuffed grass stains. One scribble belonged to Mike. I examined the T in Torrez: so simple, yet so strong, the name climbing high, determined. It was so much like the man and his personality. Looking up, I saw Mike and Iannick reappearing, our son's small mouth smeared with orange soda. Mike was beaming with pride as he carried Iannick back to me, and for a moment, nothing else mattered. This is what I had wanted so long to see—father and son, happy, together.

I grabbed the boy's pen and hurriedly wrote out my name. Danielle Gagnon Torrez. I crossed my T with Mike's on purpose. I was touching him, this time, forever. I held onto the ball for a moment, just savoring. I could not simply let go of this last piece of my life all by myself.

The boy took the ball from my hand, while I managed to hold back the tears burning my eyes. Then, I gave the boy a weak, trembling smile. His face looked confused and full of question. But he looked down at his ball and began turning it around and around.

"Gee, thanks, Mrs. Torrez!" he cried.

I turned my eyes toward the field. At this point, it took all I had to bring a hand over my head to wave at my husband. Mike was sprinting over to deep left field now and waving back. He was saying goodbye, I knew, for just a couple of weeks.

But I was saying goodbye forever.

EPILOGUE

In 1981, in October, I was at the Barbizon Hotel in Manhattan, at an exclusive party in a penthouse on the thirty-fourth floor. But inexplicably I found myself drifting away from everyone in the room and moving steadily toward a window. I brushed aside the curtain and looked out toward Central Park. The area was black and chilly, like a deep stretch of dark velvet. Then, in the distance, rising like a diamond-studded brooch, the sparkle of Yankee Stadium.

The sight instantly recalled the smell of ballpark hot dogs, the faces of the fans, and the ever-present Goodyear blimp. I could almost hear the crack of a bat, distinct and compelling, then a lusty, massive cheer. This was no ordinary October's night: it was once again World Series time in New York City.

Why was I still so drawn to all this? I had the sudden urge to pick up my coat, rush quickly from the party, hail a fast cab to the Bronx. But what would I do when I got there? Where would I go, sit, for whom would I cheer?

So much had gotten inside of me. I still turned instinctively to the sports sections when I picked up the morning paper,

237

still thought of February as the beginning of the year and October as its end. I also shivered whenever I passed a major league ballpark and grew anxious when I spied young boys with bats and gloves.

The mention of the cities I'd lived in brought instant memories: learning the game in the stands at Jarry Park, struggling in Baltimore with my new role, the fun and the warmth of Liz Mitchell in Oakland, the company of superstars in New York, and the frustration over the losses and my deteriorating marriage in Boston. Images vibrant, colorful, and too ingrained to hide away on a shelf. Thoughts also that would swell up, I suspected, eight months of every year for the rest of my life.

I threw back my head and took a strong, deep breath. I was living my life now in other ways, modeling more, raising my son alone. I'd even purchased my own house. I could make it in the outside world; I was no longer little more than a ballplayer's "fifth base." I could go on with my new life.

But gazing at Central Park and the bright, exotic brooch of Yankee Stadium in the distance, I knew also I would never be completely in control. I was addicted: I still wanted to go back there, to sit in the wives' section, to cheer with the others for my man; I still wanted to be a part of that game, of major league baseball.

And even more important, I thought: I always would.